Hedley Derenzie's work has appeared in *Nature & Health*, *The Huffington Post* and *Thought Catalog*, among other publications. She is the author of three books, including two on public speaking, and *Finding Paris* (2013), the first in her travel/romance memoir series. She divides her time between Sydney and Ubud.

For more information about the upcoming Write *Your* Way Home retreats, please go to www.hedleyderenzie.com

By the same author

Creative Keynote

Finding Paris

Write Way Home

HEDLEY DERENZIE

First published in Xoum by Brio Books in 2018

Brio Books Pty Ltd
PO Box Q324, QVB Post Office,
NSW 1230, Australia
www.briobooks.com.au

ISBN 978-1-925589-21-4 (print)
ISBN 978-1-925589-22-1 (digital)

Cataloguing-in-publication data is available from the National Library of Australia

Cover design by Brio Books Pty Ltd
Printed and bound in Australia by McPherson's Printing Group

Papers used by Brio Books are natural, recyclable products made from wood grown in sustainable forests. The manufacturing processes conform to the environmental regulations of the country of origin.

Contents

Prologue

It was still dark when I stumbled through my apartment door in the early hours of Saturday morning. I was sobbing uncontrollably, but I couldn't tell you exactly why. I couldn't tell you how many glasses of wine I'd drunk during the night. Or when I made the switch to vodka. I was in no state to remember details. I just knew it was more alcohol than my body had absorbed in years and, while it wasn't the reason, it no doubt contributed to what happened next.

I'd been hanging out at a local bar with my friend Tony and his son, Jackson. My close friend Anna had left several hours earlier. Suddenly, with my head resting on the shoulder of the bar's owner, a wave of agitation pulled me to my feet. I wanted to go home. I *needed* to go home. 'I'm off,' I slurred before stumbling onto the street where Tony and Jackson placed me in a taxi. The sound of the car door slamming shut echoed through my bones and a deep, unbounded feeling of loneliness lunged for me like a drunken date. Except there was no one with me. I was alone. Too drunk and exhausted to push the feeling away, it swallowed me whole.

When I got home, I headed straight for the bathroom. I fumbled through the medicine cabinet in search of eye make-up remover but my swollen eyes landed on an unopened bottle of Valium instead. There they remained. The bottle had been sitting in the cabinet untouched for six months after I'd seen a doctor about the dark thoughts I'd been having. I'd insisted it was nothing to worry about. I just needed something 'to take the edge off'. It wasn't depression, I tried to explain to the doctor who was hesitant about issuing a prescription. I knew what depression was, having battled through it and come out the other side in my early twenties. There was no reason for me to be depressed. I'd just returned from a holiday in India. I was excited about the future, if a little apprehensive. I still wasn't sure what I was going to do with my life, especially since writing had taken a back seat, but there was nothing to indicate that I might be depressed, and certainly not at risk of harming myself.

Loneliness, however, had become a familiar yet unwelcome guest in the seven years since the passing of my father. This feeling had slowly morphed into what I can only describe as the most intense case of homesickness. It wasn't that I wanted to die or end my life, it's that I wanted to go home. As in back to wherever it was I had come from and to wherever it was I was going once this life was over. It was hard to define, and yet the feeling was palpable, at times overwhelming. 'Of course, I would never actually do anything,' I told the doctors and therapists I spoke to. And I meant it.

I could end this all right now. I could go home tonight.

Like a high-speed train emerging from a pitch-black tunnel, the thought came out of nowhere and struck me right between my bloodshot eyes. I stood at the basin in front of the mirror. Despite my drunkenness, I knew what I was considering. But could I really do it? Could it really be this easy?

Yes. I could. It could. Finally, I could go home.

'Only half a tablet when necessary,' the doctor had said. 'And no more than one at a time.' His expression had been severe, and I had nodded solemnly. I understood. But I never followed his instructions because I never opened the bottle. Just knowing it was there, within reach, had been enough to take the edge off. Until now, when I was dangerously close to the edge, peering over.

I grabbed the bottle, pried open the lid and tipped the tablets into the palm of my hand. There were a lot. It would be enough.

Don't think about it.

I moved quickly. Leaning over the basin and catching the water in my cupped hand, I brought the liquid to my mouth and swallowed hard. The pills disappeared. All one hundred of them. Gone. Just like that. I lifted my head, my face inches from the mirror, droplets of water dripping from my chin. I stared into my wide, sad eyes.

What have I done?

I'd only ever thought about taking my life during times of intense pain. Just knowing I had options gave me a sense of control when it felt like I had none. I carried this option around with me like a card in my back pocket that I'd whip out if ever things got hard. Simply imagining checking out was enough to ease the anguish that led to having the thought in the first place. I carried this metaphorical card in the same way I kept the Valium in the cabinet. Of course, I was never meant to play the card. I was never supposed to step over the edge.

Fuck!

Fear rose quickly. The Valium was making its way through my system. This was *not* my destiny. This was not the way I was supposed to go. Yes, I was in pain, but ending my life would only be passing that pain onto others. This was not what I wanted for those whom I loved. Suffering was not supposed to be my legacy. But it was too late. The choice was out of my hands. I'd played the card. The pills were gone, along with any control I now had over the situation or what was going to happen next.

Call an ambulance.

I didn't have long. I'd pass out at any minute, after which I wouldn't be able to help myself and neither would anyone else. I had to get to my phone. Staggering down the hallway to my bedroom, I scrabbled through the piles of clothes on my bed. My heart was racing, even though I could feel my body slowing. My eyelids felt like dead weights. I found my phone and punched in the three emergency numbers. A woman answered. 'I need an ambulance,' I said, not recognising my own voice. My speech was slurred. My tone didn't match the panic I was feeling.

'What's your address?' the woman asked calmly. I felt a wave of relief when she didn't ask why. I was ashamed and embarrassed. I didn't want her to know what I had done. I didn't want anyone to know. But I didn't have time to worry about this. I forced my address out of my mouth, and somehow the woman understood. Then the line went blank. Or I did. I'm not sure which came first.

Introduction

In the night sky outside my bedroom window, a 'blue moon' shone amid a dusting of stars. It was 31 July 2015, five months after I almost ended my life. Almost.

I didn't know what a blue moon was so I sat up in bed and Googled it, hoping to find some magical and symbolic explanation. Something that would propel me into action. By some miracle, I'd been given a second chance. But five months after coming home from hospital, I still wasn't sure what I was supposed to be doing. I was just aware of how close I came to not being here.

I began searching for hope and inspiration in things like blue moons. A blue moon, by the way, is the second full moon in the month. On a symbolic level, it represents a time of transition, an opportunity to make changes. I knew I needed to do this. If only I had the motivation and energy. I was really counting on this blue moon!

It was a Friday night and, like most Friday nights, I was in bed with a book. I did a lot of staying home reading during this time. It was as if reading about other people's lives would help me forget about what I was going to do with mine. This particular evening,

I was engrossed in Cheryl Strayed's *Wild: From Lost to Found on the Pacific Crest Trail*. The book detailed her quest to walk 1100 miles across the US. I couldn't imagine willingly choosing to walk that far, but the story captivated me nonetheless. Cheryl's journey took about three months and every ounce of strength, courage and determination she possessed. She was twenty-six at the time and had fallen into an abyss of drug addiction and anonymous sex following the death of her mother, the disintegration of her family and the end of her marriage. With her life spiralling out of control, her decision to walk the 'PCT' with no training or experience was a kind of self-redemption, a way of 'walking her way back to the person her mother had raised her to be'.

Something about the story resonated with me. At thirty-seven, most of my friends were married with kids and getting on with their lives. I, on the other hand, was busy Googling 'what is a blue moon' on my Friday nights. While I wasn't engaged in any self-destructive behaviours, I wasn't doing much of anything. I was a writer who wasn't writing and my days revolved around doing whatever was necessary to get myself through to the next one. Life had become a long, monotonous plod, with the occasional interesting astrological event thrown in for good measure.

But turning the pages of Cheryl's book, I could feel something turning inside me. *Perhaps I could set myself a challenge?* Exactly what challenge was the next question. When you're feeling stuck and unmotivated, it's hard to come up with something that's going to unstick and motivate you again. Part of me couldn't be bothered. I was happy to keep reading about other people overcoming adversity. Yet something in *Wild* nudged me towards action. I had to do *something* to get myself out of the hole I was in. It needed to be something that would lift my spirits and help me rediscover my passion and purpose.

I considered buying a backpack and walking across Australia. This idea lasted about a minute before I came up with a dozen reasons why it was a bad idea. For starters, I'm not much of a camper and trekking across Australia on my own doesn't exactly spell S-A-F-E. Plus, I was still recovering from my last camping adventure when I ended up with a urinary tract infection. There's an experience I never want to repeat.

No, I had to come up with a challenge that was safer and closer to home. Ideally, something I could do from bed if necessary. As much I wanted to push myself out of my comfort zone, I didn't want to push too hard or too far. While I had built some emotional resolve over the past five months, I was still fragile. I didn't want to set myself up for failure, and I didn't want to take unnecessary risks. I needed a challenge that would help build my emotional strength and confidence, not destroy it. The challenge had to be hard, but enjoyable, too; perhaps even fun.

That's when I had an idea.

It was 11.56 pm, four minutes before the start of the new month. I sat up in bed and grabbed my notebook. With the blue moon shining above outside, I committed the idea to paper.

I will write two thousand words a day for the next thirty-one days.

I hadn't written anything in over a year. This is despite writing being pretty much the only activity in which I experience complete joy and freedom. I've had several careers over the years, but I've always thought of myself as a writer. Writing two thousand words a day would be the perfect challenge, and not just because it meant I could stay in bed. It'd both challenge me and return me to the one thing I loved doing more than anything else. I decided to call it a 'creative pilgrimage'. Rather than walking, I would write my way back to the person I was and knew myself to be.

Excitedly, I began listing some guidelines. If this was going to be a real challenge, there would need to be real guidelines. Aware of my tendency to bend, stretch and break the rules, especially if they're my own, I had to make these guidelines clear. There would be no escape routes and no short cuts. I was going to follow through on exactly what I set out to do, and that was to write two thousand words every day for the next thirty-one days. No. Matter. What.

The guidelines included starting each day with a twenty-minute meditation. I would then set an intention for the day. This was also something I had stopped doing but used to really enjoy. It was important that the two thousand words were inspired by the day's events. This challenge was about re-engaging with the present, not the past. Therefore, the writing needed to reflect this. And there was to be no rolling over of words. If I wrote more in one day, I couldn't then count those extra words the next. Each day had to stand on its own. Finally, I'd finish each day with an intention of gratitude.

To make the challenge official I signed my name at the bottom of the page. I also posted it on Facebook, figuring a public declaration would help keep me accountable should my personal signature fail, which was highly likely. I've started and abandoned lots of projects in recent years, and my word, even if it's just with myself, has lost credibility. Having family and friends as my witness would help keep me on track and committed to reaching my destination, especially when things got hard, which they inevitably would.

The challenge wasn't so much about the number of words I could write in one day; it was about doing something consistently. I hadn't done anything consistently in what seemed like years. And my self-confidence had suffered as a result. Thirty-one days might not seem like a long time, but when you've lost confidence in yourself and don't know how to get it back, it feels like a lifetime. After the events five months ago, a lifetime was the perfect length of time. Plus, it was also the number of days in August.

As the clock struck midnight, I closed my notebook and placed it on the floor. I slid back under the covers, wrapped in a haze of excitement and nervousness. Could I do this? It didn't matter whether or not I could. I had to. In a way, my life depended on it.

—

The next morning, I began my 'creative pilgrimage' and boy, did it turn out to be an adventure. The thirty-one days were unlike anything I'd imagined or experienced. Each day was a voyage into the unknown, an exploration of the concept of creativity and what it means to live a creative life. It was brilliant and beautiful. It was also one of the hardest things I've ever done. It tested me spiritually, emotionally, mentally and physically. Especially physically. On reflection, trekking across Australia might have been easier.

I didn't begin the pilgrimage with the intention of publishing a book. My focus was on following the guidelines and completing the challenge. Halfway through, I christened the pilgrimage *Write Way Home.* I loved this title because it encapsulated exactly what I was doing. I was writing my way 'home', back to who I was and wanted to be again. Only when I'd finished did I decide to turn what I had written into a manuscript. When something has a profound impact on your life, you want to share it. I wanted people to know that even when you're at your lowest, there is another way. It's the way of creation.

Turning what I had written into something worth reading wasn't easy. With no plot or complex narrative, the challenge was to bring each day together into something that was interesting and meaningful. While I wanted to remain faithful to the original diary format, I didn't want the book to be series of rambling journal entries. Therefore, I've taken some liberties and made some changes. Each day stands alone as a chapter. At the end of each chapter I've included one central idea that captures the experience of the day. In the end, what took thirty-one days to write has taken over twenty drafts and two years to publish.

Write Way Home is a story about returning to a meaningful and authentic life via a daily creative practice. In my case, it was writing, although for others it might be something else. Creation is, after all, expressed in infinite ways. You don't have to be a writer to derive value and meaning from this book. It's for anyone who's looking for more inspiration – and who can't wait for that next blue moon.

Hedley Derenzie, 2018

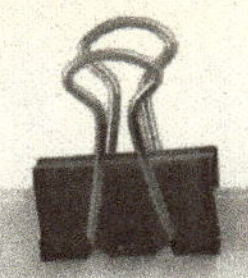

Daily Creative Commitment

1. Twenty-minute meditation

2. Recite morning intention

3. Write two thousand words inspired by the events within each twenty-four-hour period

4. Recite evening intention

5. Repeat for thirty-one consecutive days

Daily Intentions

These intentions have been adapted from the spiritual teachings of True Divine Nature.

Morning Intention

I accept that today has already been destined to be one of the most miraculous, healing, clarifying and transformative days of my entire life. I allow my physical, emotional and mental bodies along with my energy fields to instantaneously heal, miraculously transform and spontaneously awaken into the purity, wholeness and perfection of my soul's highest potential. In knowing it is so I allow it to be revealed, here as I am now.

And so it is.

Evening Intention

Thank you for this day, a day that has been one of the most miraculous, healing, clarifying and transformative days of my entire life. Thank you for the instantaneous healings, miraculous transformations and spontaneous awakenings of my physical, emotional and mental bodies along with my energy fields, into the purity, wholeness and perfection of my soul's highest potential. And in knowing it is so and that the Truth of my Divinity has been revealed, I surrender into sleep with a loving and grateful heart.

And so it is.

Part I - Commitment

From Latin *committere* 'to unite, connect, combine; to bring together'.

Day 1

Start where you are

It's four o'clock in the afternoon and I haven't written a single word. Not on the page, at least. There are plenty of words in my head, circling like a flock of confused seagulls looking for somewhere to land. Despite doing my best to help them, so far I've come up with a bunch of reasons for them not to, mainly because I'm not sure where or how to start. Of course, I will start. Eventually. I have to because I'm committed and there's no going back now. Right?

Um, well ...

The chance of failure is high. I know this based on the countless creative projects I've started and then abandoned in recent years. Like the erotic novel I began writing six months ago and stopped at the precise point in the story when the two protagonists moved in for a passionate kiss. The idea of writing about 'tongues entwining' – along with other body parts – was enough to drive me into the cupboard in search of the cleaning equipment. When my apartment started to look like a page out of a real estate magazine, I knew this wasn't about cleaning. I was procrastinating. Again.

As a writer, I have become proficient at *not* writing. This persistent non-writing and the sense of creative failure that goes with it is what drove me to sit up in bed last night and embark on this two-thousand-words-a-day adventure. *Two thousand words for the next thirty-one days? What on earth were you thinking? You won't make it through the first week. You're begging to fail. Why do this to yourself?*

I'm calling it a 'pilgrimage' because I'm starting what feels like an impossible journey even though I'm not going anywhere. Except down the hill to Earl's. Earl's is my local café and second home based on the amount of time I spend there (not writing, obviously). The café is at the bottom of a steep hill, a short four-minute stroll or ten-minute workout, depending on which direction you're heading. Across the road from the café is the beach. Sitting there drinking coffee is a truly beautiful thing. You have a lovely view of the ocean – perfect for procrastinating. Not that I'll be doing any of that today. The times they are a-changin', baby. I hope so, anyway.

I check my phone: 4.07 pm. Plenty of time, I think, even though I've been saying this all day. I need to stop saying this and start writing. I have an idea of what I want to write, but this is the problem. An idea doesn't equal words on the page. An idea is not the end of the creative process – this has been my attitude of late. At some point there has to be action. I need to take the idea I have in my head and do something with it.

Charging down the hill with my laptop under my arm I decide to start with the appointment I had this morning with Boris, my Russian chiropractor. I'll write about how he told me in his thick accent that I was 'God's pencil' who 'vill wrrrite God's storrry'. I'll omit the bit about how my ego loves hearing him say this. *Yes, that's right, people, I'm God's pencil and I am here to write something very,*

very important. Once my fingers are moving, I'm sure the rest of the words will take care of themselves.

I greet Earl, the café owner, before sitting down at my favourite table in a subdued corner at the rear of the café. From this vantage point I can take in the view while remaining discreet. Although, I remind myself, I'm not here to take in the view. I'm here to write. Two thousand words to be exact. I place my laptop on the table and position my fingers over the keyboard. Finally, I'm ready to begin ...

'Where did you come from?'

I look up to see a man standing in front of me. He's wearing jeans, a shabby grey T-shirt and a toothy smile.

'I'm sorry?' I ask, even though I'm not. He's the one interrupting my creative flow – that hasn't quite started yet.

'I just went to pay my bill and I turn around and there's a beautiful woman sitting next to my table. Where were you an hour ago?'

'Oh,' I say, with an awkward laugh. 'Thank you. I'm just here to do some writing.' I bow my head, returning my focus to the screen, hoping he'll get the message.

'Ah, so you're a writer?'

I slowly raise my head and give a reluctant nod.

'So am I,' the man says cheerfully.

Oh, please no!

There's a black notebook on the table suggesting he's telling the truth. 'You know,' he says, 'I think my writing session would have been a lot easier if you'd arrived an hour earlier. Do you mind if I join you?'

'Um, well, actually ...' *Yes, I mind. Go away.*

'Wonderful,' he says, with his wide, toothy grin. He sits back down at the table he was supposed to be leaving.

I force a smile, and then remember: *I'm on a creative pilgrimage.* If a slightly creepy guy who turns out to be a writer appears out of nowhere and wants to chat, isn't it my duty to roll with it? The whole point of this exercise is to reacquaint myself with the magic of life. In other words, to stop trying to control everything and open myself up to living differently. I close the lid of my computer.

'So what do you write?' I ask, shifting my body to face him.

'I'm a screenwriter. I've just been working on a script – a romantic comedy. I sold it to Universal Pictures and I have to get it finished. I'm on a pretty tight deadline.'

'Really?' I ask with a touch of scepticism.

'Uh-huh. Well, actually, I sold three scripts. Right now I'm working on the first one.'

I scan his face for a flicker of an eyelid, a twitch of the mouth, a droplet of sweat on his forehead. Something to suggest dishonesty. But his face doesn't move, other than for the toothy smile which is still very much in place. Perhaps he really *has* sold three scripts to Universal Pictures. Confusion sets in.

'So you're telling me that you just rocked up to Universal and signed a deal to write three scripts?'

He nods. 'There's a little more to it but essentially that's about right.'

I can't believe this guy. This in itself is interesting. When did I become sceptical of other people's success? I decide to change my attitude by believing everything he's telling me, especially the part about just having sold three scripts. Even if he hasn't, it's a good story. If he can do it, why can't I?

'So how did you end up writing scripts and selling them to Universal?' I ask.

'Ah,' he says, clearly hoping I'd ask this question. 'Well, I'm a teacher ...'

'English?'

'No, I'm Irish.'

I laugh. 'No, I mean are you an English teacher?'

'Ah, no. I teach film and theatre.'

I nod. 'Got it.'

'I'm Christian, by the way.' He holds out his hand.

'I'm spiritual,' I say, holding out mine.

'What?'

I shake my head and laugh, figuring it will take too long to explain. 'Hedley,' I say instead.

'Well, hello, Hedley. About five years ago I divorced my wife and gave her everything except for $50,000, which I kept for myself. I thought, "Right, what am I going to do now?" I loved teaching but I needed to do something else. And then I thought, "I'm going to be a writer."' He pauses for a moment before leaning in as if about to whisper an important secret in my ear. I watch him warily, making sure he doesn't lean in too closely. 'But you know? I'm actually not a writer.'

'You're not?' *Ah-ha! I was right! He was telling a porky!*

'I'm a storyteller,' he says, leaning back and appearing very proud of the mystery he's just revealed. 'And there's a difference.'

I nod while desperately wanting to call out, 'I'm not a writer, either! I'm a storyteller too!' But I refrain, allowing Christian to continue his sermon.

'So I thought, "What do I have to do to be a writer? I have to do a writing course." But there are so many out there and I didn't want to do just any old one. If you're going to be a writer, you have to go to the best. So, after researching all the writing programs in America, I decided on Disney.'

'Disney has a writing course?'

Christian nods. 'They do for screenwriters. I showed them my stories and talked them into taking me on. I then paid $18,000 to learn that I don't need to do a writing course that's going to teach me how to write like everyone else. After that I realised I didn't need to study writing; I just needed to ask the right questions of the right people.'

'What do you mean?'

'I went to see James Cameron speak at an event in Hollywood and you know what I did?'

I shake my head, suddenly interested in hearing what Christian has to say.

'Rather than asking him the same questions that every other writer asks, I said, "I'm a storyteller and you need to spend five minutes with me over coffee to find out what I can share with you."'

'You told James Cameron that he needs to spend five minutes with you?'

Christian nods. 'Remember, it's all about interest. Once you have someone's interest, you then have to figure out a way to keep it. Imagine how many times a day James Cameron gets asked out for coffee.'

'A lot.'

'Exactly. So, if I want five minutes of his time, I have to go about it differently. It might sound arrogant, but if you want to be the best, you have to think like the best. You have to give them the unexpected.'

'So did you have coffee with James Cameron?'

Again, Christian nods. 'He was intrigued, so he agreed.'

'Wow. I'm impressed. What did he say?'

'He said writing isn't about word quantity, it's about picture quality. Write what you see, describe it in detail and make the picture as clear as you can for the reader. Tell the best story you can and tell it as clearly and efficiently as possible.'

'I love that.'

'Me too. Writing is storytelling. We're just telling stories. And stories are simply pictures painted with words.'

I nod, grateful for this conversation. It's clear why I haven't started my two thousand words. This conversation needed to happen first. I suddenly realise my creative pilgrimage has begun and I have no idea how this next month is going to play out.

Christian asks me what I'm working on and so I tell him about my creative pilgrimage. 'That sounds wonderful,' he says. 'What are your two thousand words for today going to be about?'

'I think this conversation is a good place to start. Would you mind if I wrote about you and our serendipitous meeting?'

'Sure. Just make sure you change my name. And make me younger and sexier.'

'Deal,' I say, laughing.

Christian slides out from behind the table and slings his laptop bag over his shoulder. 'You know what's truly serendipitous about meeting you today?'

'What?'

'Every morning I start my day with an intention and today that intention was to be inspired. Today I set the intention that I would meet a writer who would inspire me to start writing that book I've always wanted to write.'

I stare at him. 'Really? That's incredible because that's how I started my day as well.'

'A lot of people talk about doing something but they never actually do it. You're doing it and now you've inspired me to go and do it too. Starting is often the hardest part.'

I smile. 'Tell me about it.'

As Christian turns to leave, I notice his black notebook still on the table. 'Hey, don't forget this,' I say, holding it out for him.

He turns around and pretends to have a heart attack. 'My God,' he gasps. 'Can't forget that.'

As I hand the notebook over, it falls open to a page filled with black, incomprehensible scribbles. 'What's all that?' I ask.

Christian smiles, placing the notebook down in front of me. He points to the scribbles. 'That's what a $40-million-dollar movie looks like.'

I stare at him, confused.

'Remember, Hedley, studios don't buy screenplays and people don't buy books. They buy stories. They buy the way those stories make them *feel*.'

I realise the scribbles are the outline of his story, the one he's sold to Universal Pictures for an exorbitant amount of money.

'At the end of the day,' he says, 'success is very simple.'

Insight of the Day

Start where you are. It doesn't matter where that is. Just start somewhere.

Day 2

For bloomin' sake, just do it

I wake bathed in sweat. Before my eyes have even opened, my mind is off and running. *What if that was it? What if that unexpected meeting with Christian was as good as it gets? What if absolutely nothing of any consequence happens for the rest of the month and everything I write from this moment on is just one long, meandering ramble about nothing in particular? What if I've already run out of things to say?*

Surely I can't have run out of things to say. It's only the second day. But it is possible that by setting myself to write two thousand words a day for the next month, I've set myself up to fail. By 'fail' I mean give up and wander off in search of something better to do. It doesn't even have to be something 'better'. Just something 'else' is often enough. It wouldn't be the first time I've done this. Usually, it's around the halfway mark of whatever it is I'm working on at the time. Although sometimes I don't even make it that far.

Over the last twelve months, I've started at least twelve different books. All of them bestsellers in the making; none of them compelling enough to continue beyond the initial outline. There's always another 'amazing' idea hanging out in the wings of my imagination, waiting for a break in my concentration before launching itself into my consciousness and stealing my enthusiasm away from the 'amazing' idea I'm currently working on. The next idea is always so much more exciting. Until there's an even better one.

I can see how this idea-hopping has led to feelings of discouragement, disappointment and defeat. The less I create, the less creative I feel, and the less enthused about life I become. Laziness, frustration and procrastination set in. And who wants to be that person? When you start to become the person you least want to hang out with, that's when it's time to pack your bags and head cross-country. Or stay home and commit to writing two thousand words a day. Whatever takes your fancy.

My greatest fear is that this creative pilgrimage is just another 'amazing' idea that will soon turn out to be not so amazing – usually, around the time things start to get hard – which at some point they will. I fear that if I can't even finish this creative project, what hope is there for me as a writer? I'll be jettisoned back into the creative wilderness, left to spend my days wandering aimlessly through a forest of old and dilapidated ideas that were once so rich with possibility had I just had the commitment to see them through. The fact of the matter is I *have* to finish this. I'm not sure what will become of me if I don't.

I set off towards Clovelly, along the coastal path beside the old Waverley Cemetery. The day is overcast and windy and I can hear the sound of the ocean slamming against the rocks below. I increase my pace in a bid to exhaust the thoughts raging through my mind. *Can I really do this? What have I set myself up for? Will I do this? What will happen if I don't?*

Straying from the path, I walk across the grassy clearing filled with dogs scampering around in arse-smelling circles towards an empty bench overlooking the ocean. I take a seat and pull my notebook from the side pocket of my yoga pants. I've been carrying a notebook around for years, although this is the first time I've taken one on my morning walk. If I'm going to write two thousand words inspired by each twenty-four-hour period, I need to be prepared. A writer's workbench is the world. It's important to always carry the right tools. Inspiration can and often does strike at any time.

This particular notebook was given to me by my father after one of his trips to the Guggenheim Museum in New York. Dad loved art and enjoyed surrounding himself and his home with it. It must be fifteen years ago that he gave me this particular notebook. It's been sitting in the drawer all that time, along with an ever-growing pile of similar notebooks, waiting to be plucked from the stack. Having it with me gives me the comforting sense my father is on this adventure too. The thought makes me smile.

It's been six years since he died. I wonder what he would say about this creative pilgrimage. He'd probably smirk to which I would ask, 'Why are you smirking?' 'I'm not smirking,' he'd say, which would make me angry. He'd then offer an equally annoying piece of advice such as, 'Just keep your feet on the ground' or 'Just go easy' or 'No need to get ahead of yourself'. I've been known to fly off with the fairies, go hard and get way ahead of myself, a combination that usually leads to falling in a heap.

I run my fingers over the notebook's smooth cover. It features the painting, *The Football Players*, by Henri Rousseau. On the inside cover is a brief description of the artist.

Henri Rousseau (1844–1910)

A Sunday painter who only began to paint seriously in his forties, Henri Rousseau endured the art-historical misfortune of being a working-

class late bloomer. While to many he seemed to possess little natural talent, his unsentimental, haunting images nonetheless drew the attention of a literary and artistic group hungry for fresh recruits. During his lifetime he became something of a sensation within the Parisian art scene. Canvases such as The Football Players *have been interpreted as Rousseau's quirky attempts to depict modern times.*

From now on I will call my notebooks 'Henri'. After all, they're alive with my thoughts and ideas, responsible for carrying around my words and musings. It's therefore fitting they have the respect of a name. By naming and numbering them accordingly, they take on a certain regal nature. Henri 1st. Henri 2nd. Henri 8th. And so on.

I take comfort in knowing that Henri (the artist, not the notebook) was a late bloomer. My father was also a late bloomer, only discovering his passion for writing in the weeks leading up to his death. He would scribble his thoughts and poems on scraps of paper, his eyes sparkling, excited to read to me what he had written. He was good, and I told him so. I'm glad he got to experience the joy of writing before he died.

I notice a group of beginner scuba divers. I know they're beginners from the way they waddle awkwardly along the path towards the water, their bodies bent over by the weight of the equipment on their backs. One hunched-over woman is shuffling sideways and appears to be questioning the entire exercise. It's tiring just watching her. Moments later, the group is scattered about in the tumbling ocean, bobbing around like little black croutons in a large, dark soup.

We are all in various stages of bloom. Whether we're scuba diving or painting or writing, our lives unfold in their unique way. Some will bloom earlier and faster than others, but it's better to bloom late than not at all.

Insight of the Day

It's never too late to listen to your creative urgings.

Day 3

Perfection versus completion

I stand on top of the cliff overlooking Bondi Beach compiling a list of reasons why I'm already a failure and why I don't have what it takes to make it as a writer. To make matters worse, my new G-string is riding up my arse in ways it really shouldn't, considering the amount of money I paid for it. It's not a good start to the day, the third day of my creative pilgrimage.

Part of me knows these thoughts are not true. Except for the part about the G-string. This part is very true, and I yank it out of my bum for the fourteenth time. As for being a failure who'll never make it as a writer? I suspect that's my ego's way of getting out of this challenge. Believing I'm going to fail before I've even really begun is the same as saying, 'Why bother? May as well head to the beach instead.' Although it's understandable. There's bound to be some hard work involved in this process, something I've been known to weasel my way out of on occasion.

I know my self-worth isn't dependent on my achievements, or anything else, for that matter. Therapy has taught me this. My worth as a person has nothing to do with whether I finish this creative challenge or write a book. My existence alone is sufficient evidence of my worth. I know this but sometimes I have a hard time believing it. Like now. I, therefore, have three options:

1. I can continue torturing myself at the risk of sliding into a pit of despair that could potentially last for days, if not weeks. Note to self: this option is not helpful and should only be considered as a last resort.

2. I can accept the uncomfortable fact that right now I feel awful and believe I'm a failure and just keep putting one foot, or rather one word, in front of the other.

3. Surely there's a third option? The first two options suck.

While Option 2 isn't the most attractive option, it's the right one. Sometimes well-meaning attempts to change or fix or transform or heal or ignore an uncomfortable feeling only intensify and prolong it. Like a parent faced with a screaming child, there are times when all you can do is let them scream. You can't give in to their every whim. Eventually they will tire. My mind in its current state is the equivalent of a screaming child, and the only way to handle it is to let it wear itself out. Eventually it will. At least I hope it will.

I was expecting this internal revolt. I just didn't expect it to happen on Day 3. It's slightly premature. But then this challenge is already turning out to be full of unexpected surprises. In order for a challenge to be a challenge we need to overcome some difficulty or adversity. More often than not, that difficulty or adversity lies within. Human beings are fantastic at being their worst enemy. We place unnecessary pressures on ourselves to be perfect even though life is anything but. Life rarely plays out in straight lines and let's be honest, who wants to play a game where you already know the ending? Okay, so I feel awful today. Life isn't perfect and not every day is going to feel great. Imperfection is okay because life is imperfect. And so am I.

With that little pep talk out of the way, I can get on with accepting just how imperfect I'm feeling right now. Although I'm not exactly doing that. Rather, I'm accepting that I don't accept it, which is better than not accepting anything. Having satisfactorily confused myself I've forgotten about feeling like a failure. It's a small win. I dislodge my undies from my bum once more and turn towards home.

With my eyes on the ground, I notice five words painted in black along the path. I stop to read them. *Commitment. Ambition. Determination. Sacrifice. Courage.* I sense they're some kind of creative guideposts and I whip Henri (my notebook) out to jot them down. As I walk on, I repeat the words silently like a marching mantra: *Commitment. Ambition. Determination. Sacrifice. Courage. Commitment. Ambition. Determination ...*

'Oh my God!' I say, suddenly looking up to find myself about to walk straight into my friend Emma. She's with her husband Brett who's carrying their two-year-old daughter Ava in a BabyBjörn. Also with them are their huskies, Buster and Rupert. 'I almost didn't see you.'

'I know,' says Emma with a laugh. 'I've been waving at you from all the way back there, but you were deep in thought.'

'What a nice surprise.' I give each of them a kiss and a hug. 'I never run into you guys along here.'

'We thought we'd get out of the house. Ava was awake all night so we're both exhausted.'

'Sorry to hear that.' I lean over to give Ava a kiss. She blinks away the sun and turns her cheek, snuggling into her father's chest. 'Where are you headed?'

'We're going to Tama for a coffee. Come with us?'

Tamarama is the next beach along with an outdoor café.

'Sure. I'd love to.' I offer to take the two dogs from Brett, and he hands me the leads.

I met Emma and Brett last summer. Ava was just a baby. One day, while sitting on the beach, Brett approached and asked if I would mind keeping an eye on Ava for five minutes while he took a dip. The next time this happened, Brett and I began exchanging greetings and eventually conversations. I met Emma soon after and a friendship quickly developed. I catch up with them for a coffee at Earl's every other week.

On any other occasion, I would have seen running into Emma and Brett along the coastal path as nothing more than a pleasant surprise. Today, however, the encounter seems profound. Within my creative adventure every moment contains the seed of inspiration for those two thousand words.

'So how was your weekend?' I ask Emma as we sit down at one of the tables overlooking the horseshoe-shaped beach. I pull Henri from the side pocket of my pants. Ava has waddled over to a group of children who are playing in the sand.

'Great,' Emma says, her eyes fixed on her daughter. 'We went down to Melbourne to visit a friend of mine. He's an artist.'

'What kind of artist?'

'He paints these geometrical shapes. They're incredible. He could be very successful but he has this "I'm not good enough" belief that gets in the way.'

I laugh. 'I can relate to that, especially now that I'm on this creative pilgrimage.'

Emma read my declaration on Facebook and was one of the many people to offer an encouraging comment. 'Well, it's a big commitment you've made,' she says, taking a sip of her latte. 'I'd be freaking out. I always think of creativity as like a long-term relationship. It takes work. It's not always easy, but you have to stick with it. You can have all the best ideas in the world, but if you can't commit to any of them, they'll never become anything.'

'So true,' I say with a nod. 'I'm always jumping from one thing to the next. It's like I'm having these creative flings when what I really want is a long-term relationship.'

'Sounds like you're suffering from a case of creative FOMO.'

I laugh. 'Oh my God, that's *exactly* what I'm suffering from. I'm afraid that if I commit to one idea, I'll miss out on an even better one.'

'But then you end up missing out on all of them because you're never able to stick with anything long enough to create what it is you really want – which is that long-term relationship.'

'True again,' I say, shaking my head. 'I'm a FOMO-er. So what's the answer? How do I stop?'

'Just decide on something and stick to it.'

'I only figured that out after I divorced my first wife,' says Brett, joining us at the table.

'What happened?' I ask.

'I was this Peter Pan type of guy, jumping from person to person and project to project until I realised it wasn't a fulfilling way to live.'

'How did you work that out?'

'Therapy. A *lot* of therapy.' Brett laughs. 'Relationships are hard, especially long-term ones, because you have to keep showing up even when the going gets tough, which it always does ...'

'And they can get really boring ...' Emma adds.

'Thanks,' says Brett, feigning hurt before laughing again.

'I don't mean *you're* boring,' Emma says, squeezing his arm and leaning over to give him a kiss. 'But there are times when things get hard and boring, but you stick with it because you love the person and you know the pluses outweigh the minuses. That's what you've got to remember. Committing to something doesn't mean you're missing out on something else; it means you're gaining what you ultimately want.'

'This is good stuff,' I say, scribbling down as much of the conversation as I can.

Brett's phone rings and he jumps out of his seat to take the call.

'I can't believe that just came out of my mouth,' says Emma, chuckling. 'That was good.'

'It was. That's why I'm writing it down. By the way, when are you going to get back into your designing?' Before becoming a mum, Emma worked as an architect.

'I don't know,' she says, her attention still on Ava who's playing with her new friends. 'I'd like to, but right now I just don't have the time. Or maybe that's an excuse.'

'Is it?'

Emma shrugs. 'Ava's still young.' She pauses, gazing at her daughter before adding, 'It's been so long since I've done anything. I've probably lost a bit of confidence. I don't know if I'd be any good anymore.'

I nod. Perhaps fear and doubt are just part of the creative experience. They certainly seem to pervade the mind of almost every artist I know.

'Well, I'm sure you'll know when the time is right to get back into it,' I say.

Emma smiles while I check the time on my phone and decide I

should probably get going. As much as I've enjoyed the morning, I have some words to write.

—

That evening, I join my friend Grace at the Sydney Theatre to see a play about love and relationships. I met Grace on a yoga retreat several years ago, recognising her face immediately from the several popular Australian soapies in which she once starred. Grace is an actor who, like Emma, put her career to the side to raise a family. She'd called earlier in the day with a spare ticket, and as I'm on a creative pilgrimage, I grabbed it gratefully, even though I would have grabbed it anyway.

As the play materialises under the stage lights and gaze of a packed house, I quickly become confused. It has no storyline or narrative to speak of, and after an hour or so, I still have no idea what's going on. Actors run on and off the stage, performing scenes consisting of snippets of conversations that have no connection to each other. I keep waiting for the moment when suddenly everything makes sense, but when the lights go up and the actors take their final bows, I figure that moment is never coming. Eventually, Grace leans forward and asks, 'What on earth was that?'

I shrug, grateful not to be the only clueless person in the audience. The experience has highlighted the importance of a narrative, something the audience can hold onto and make sense of. While the play might have resembled a patchwork blanket loosely stitched together for no particular purpose, it was still a finished piece of art. The playwright had an idea – if an incomprehensible one – and enough discipline to transform it into a finished product with real actors performing in a real theatre in front of a real audience. That in itself is worthy of applause.

Insight of the Day

Making a commitment to one thing doesn't mean missing out on something else. It means working towards creating what it is you ultimately want.

Day 4

Stick to it!

Cleo is sitting alone at the communal table in the centre of the café, which doubles as a second-hand bookstore, when I arrive. Her head is tilted over a book and I creep up behind her, grabbing her shoulders in an attempt to give her a friendly fright. She doesn't flinch, just turns around calmly and smiles.

'Well, aren't you relaxed,' I say, leaning down to give her a kiss on the cheek. 'You obviously had a great holiday.'

Cleo's smile quickly turns into a scowl.

'Okay, so I'm sensing there's a story there. Let me order a coffee, and then I want to hear all about it.'

Cleo and I met when we worked as reluctant promotional models in our early twenties. We bonded over our distaste for the job which involved standing around at corporate events dressed in too-tight outfits while handing out products we didn't believe in or care about to drunken men. When no one was looking, we'd go in search of a bottle of wine before drinking and laughing ourselves into the night. After the company went bust, possibly not helped by our antics, Cleo went on to have three kids and lead a family-centric life and I, well, didn't. Our different life paths have meant that, unfortunately, we don't get to see as much of each other these days. I return to the table with my order number and pull up a chair, eager to hear her story. 'So tell me everything.'

'You know how we were going to see Emery's family in Germany?' I nod. She's referring to her husband Emery and their three kids, Bella, Jack and Piper. 'Well, I didn't want to go, so Emery and I made a deal. If we were going to spend three weeks with his family, I wanted a week in a tropical resort where I could lie by the pool and drink cocktails.'

'That sounds like a fair trade.'

'Have you met Emery's family?' asks Cleo. 'It wasn't even *close* to being a fair trade. Those three weeks in Germany were hell. There were fifteen of us sleeping in a three-bedroom house, and my brother-in-law's kids are a nightmare. And I mean a *nightmare*. The older son is a serial killer in the making. I barely slept the whole time because I was so worried that at any moment this kid was going to lose it and start stabbing one of my kids in a wild frenzy.'

Cleo's deadpan delivery is irresistible, and I can feel the smile cracking across my face.

'I'm not kidding,' she continues, her expression serious. 'This kid wasn't normal. I had to be on guard the whole time because all the kids were hanging out together and I seriously didn't know what he was capable of. I couldn't wait for those three weeks to end so I could get to the tropical resort and drink cocktails and sleep without having to worry about my family being murdered.'

'So what happened?'

'Well, the kids survived, thank goodness. And then Emery, God bless him, booked us into a resort in Dubai on the way home.'

'Interesting choice for a tropical island holiday.'

'I told him I wanted a luxury hotel, hot weather and a massive pool. So he went and found the biggest hotel in the world in the hottest place on earth with the biggest pool you've ever seen.'

I throw my head back in laughter.

'We arrived in Dubai in 47-degree heat, and since I was still recovering from Emery's psychopathic family, I headed straight for the pool where I ordered a mojito. The waiter looked at me and said, "I'm sorry, but we are not currently serving any alcohol." I just stared at him. The words were not computing in my head.'

'Why weren't they serving alcohol?'

'It was Ramadan! It's the only time they don't serve alcohol there, not even to tourists. You should have seen the look I gave Emery when I got back to the room. The poor man was terrified.'

'Oh God, Cleo,' I say, still laughing.

'It was the worst holiday of my life. I'm still recovering. But hey, enough about me. I saw on Facebook you're doing some kind of creative challenge. How's it going?'

'I'm only four days into it, so I don't want to get ahead of myself, but so far so good. I'm writing again, and that's the main thing. Although the chance of me getting bored and giving up are high so I don't want to say too much in case I jinx myself.'

'I wouldn't have even made it this far, so you're already my hero.'

'That's very kind. But I do have this niggling fear that at any moment my mind will declare this a complete waste of time and I'll just give up. Right now, my enthusiasm is at its peak, but I know that will change the minute it starts getting hard. The test will be when I hit the halfway mark.'

'One day at a time, as they say.'

I nod, taking a sip of coffee. 'It helps having people ask me how it's going. It keeps me accountable. And everyone is being so encouraging and supportive. I guess social media isn't a complete waste of time, after all.'

'It is in my household.'

'Ha. So how's your business going? Are you still doing your building inspections?'

These days Cleo is a building biologist – a far cry from promotional modelling. She goes into people's houses armed with a bunch of devices that measure toxins. She's then able to help them make their houses healthier.

'It's going really well. I've just picked up a new client, Karen, who lives in this huge mansion overlooking the ocean. I'm seeing her this week although I'm hoping she doesn't cancel after the recent débâcle.'

'What recent débâcle?'

'She threw this big fancy dress party a few weeks ago, and of course, I misunderstood the theme.'

'Oh God,' I giggle. 'What did you do?'

'The dress code was James Bond. So naturally, I'm thinking fancy dress ... I'll go as a martini glass.'

'Only you could come to that conclusion. I love it. How do you dress as a martini glass?'

'Well,' says Cleo, now laughing along with me, 'I took one of Piper's hula-hoops, wrapped it with clear cellophane, and wore it around my waist over a black bodysuit. For my olive, I stole Jack's football, painted it green and stabbed a stick through it. Emery went as James *Bondi* – half tux, half beach bum. Honestly, I thought we were going to win best dressed. But when Karen opened the door I knew something was wrong. Everyone was dressed in black-tie suits and expensive-looking designer gowns. Karen gave me a very strange look, invited us in and spent the rest of the night avoiding us. At one point, I put my olive down on the couch, only to later find it hidden in a cupboard.'

'I love it! Seriously, I love that you do stuff like that. You're *my* hero.'

'Emery looked even more uncomfortable than me. I did think about running away. I was so embarrassed. But then I thought, "Who cares, I put a lot of effort into this outfit." So we stayed, and I got very drunk, which of course helped. By the end of the night, I convinced myself that everyone was secretly jealous of my outfit.'

'I bet they were,' I say, catching my breath. While Cleo is passionate about ridding people's homes of toxins, she is equally passionate about consuming them herself, mainly (but not limited to) alcohol.

'So anyway, based on the fact that Karen hasn't cancelled yet, I'm assuming she still likes me.'

'Of course she still likes you. Who wouldn't? How many people have the gumption to turn up to a black-tie event dressed as a martini glass?'

'Only stupid people who can't read invitations correctly.'

'I think it's inspiring. You backed yourself creatively and put yourself out there. That takes guts.'

Cleo smiles. 'Thank you. I appreciate that at least one person appreciates my efforts.'

Half an hour later I hug my friend goodbye and head back out into the morning sunshine. As I wander to the car, I think more about Cleo's story. As funny and entertaining as it was, it's also inspiring. It's not easy to expose yourself creatively. Doing so means risking judgment and criticism. Being creative takes courage. It's a personal reminder. This is the kind of artist I want to be.

—

After a few hours of writing, I head out again to grab some lunch from another local spot, Smith's. Matt, the owner, pulls up a stool next me while I wait for my order. 'So, Hedley, tell me, what's your definition of success?'

In the few months I've been coming to Smith's, I've not known Matt to be much of a conversationalist. 'Where did that question come from?' I ask playfully.

'We've been talking about it all morning,' he says, gesturing to Hendrix, the effervescent waiter bouncing from table to table. 'I'm keen to hear your take.'

I think about the question for a moment, and my thoughts turn to my conversation with Cleo. 'You know, a few years ago I might have said it was having a publisher and selling a lot of books, but it's not that.' A vision of Cleo dressed as a martini glass in the middle of a roomful of people in eveningwear flashes through my mind. 'I would say success is doing what you love regardless of what people think. It's knowing who you are and being true to that.'

Matt nods, sipping his coffee.

'What about you?' I ask. 'What's your definition?'

'Happiness,' he says with authority.

'Even though he's never happy,' calls out Hendrix from the kitchen.

'This is true,' says Matt.

'Then how can happiness be your measure of success if you're never happy? By your definition, you can never be successful.'

'Exactly,' says Matt. 'That's what keeps me motivated. There's always more to do and achieve. If you're happy, what else is there?'

It's an interesting way of defining success, even though it's not how I would define it. I recognise that feeling of discontent only too well. The idea I somehow have to achieve more usually leaves me feeling like my efforts aren't good enough. Consequently, I end up believing *I'm* not good enough. And that's not a healthy state of mind.

'I'm happy in other areas of my life – my family, my partner, my hobbies,' Matt continues. 'But with work, I always want to achieve more, be better. It wouldn't matter if I owned a hundred cafés; I'd always want more. That wanting more makes me happy.'

'What about you, Hendrix?' I ask as he glides by. 'What's your definition of success?'

Hendrix stops and performs a little pirouette. 'Babe, I was born successful. The moment I came out of my mother's womb, my job was done. I mean, look at me!' He uses both hands to showcase himself as if he were the grand prize on a game show. The kitchen bell chimes and he spins off again. 'But seriously,' he says, returning to the conversation a second later with three plates balanced on his arm. 'Success is a given. We're here to enjoy ourselves. When you're healthy, you have a roof over your head, food on the table and love in your heart, what more could you want? That's success, man.'

I couldn't agree more.

—

Later that evening I go to the Sydney Theatre for the second night in a row, this time to see a performance of *The Present* starring Cate Blanchett. The tickets were a gift from my mum. We arrive to find the seats tucked up the back where it's virtually impossible to hear anything happening on stage. We spend the entire evening leaning forward and cupping our ears. And while I miss most of the dialogue, there is one line in the play which I manage to catch. The husband and wife are arguing about another woman. Before storming off stage, the wife turns to her husband and yells, 'Make your mind up and stick to it!'

The words echo through the theatre. I catch hold of them. These are words I want to remember, along with so many of the conversations I've had today. I know they'll help me the next time I start doubting what I'm doing and why I'm doing it. Rather than answering such questions I can say, 'Because I made up my mind and now I'm sticking to it!'

Insight of the Day

Make up your mind to do something. Ideally, something you love. Stick to it. And don't be afraid to make a fool of yourself in the process.

Day 5

Prepare to be inconvenienced

It's Day 5 and I'm on my way to meet Grace at the theatre. This will make it three nights in a row. Unprecedented. The last time I went to the theatre three times in one week was never. I'm convinced it has something to do with this challenge. All this creative energy churning through me is whipping itself into physical matter, which in this case happens to be free theatre tickets, which is wonderful. Grace had once again called at the last minute with a spare and, once again, I grabbed it.

Unfortunately, Day 5 began with someone drilling into a wall next to my head at seven in the morning, resulting in an overwhelming aversion to writing. If there was one thing I woke up *not* wanting to do today, this was it. The confidence and exuberance experienced yesterday had magically evaporated overnight.

I knew this day was coming – the day I'd wake up and think 'I'm over it', the day when I just couldn't be arsed, the day I would give up – I just didn't think it would come so soon. It's only Day 5. Of course, it's not the first time I've woken up and felt like this. In the past, these are the days when I succumb. These are the days when I don't write. This would be why I haven't been able to manage to keep to a daily writing practice. This day always comes. I wake up, I don't feel like writing, so I don't.

Today, however, I can't do that. I've made a *commitment*.

Commitment, I've decided, equals inconvenience. The inconvenience of doing something I don't feel like doing but have to do because I've made a commitment. This is what separates the fling from the long-term relationship. In the past, the moment I've not been in the *mood* to do something is the moment I stopped. I'd wander off in search of something more convenient to do. That is, more fun and interesting and, ultimately, pleasurable. Our mood, however, is just another word for 'ego'. Therefore, the me that didn't want to write was just my ego (bless her cotton socks). Interestingly, this insight miraculously cured my resistance to writing, transforming it into the energy I needed to get those words down. Unfortunately, I didn't have this insight until much later in the day.

Instead, for most of the morning, I succumbed. Thankfully, I had arranged to meet a friend for a coffee, enabling my procrastination to continue. My friend Jodie had her twelve-month-old son Max with her and was wrestling a plastic toy out of his little hand when I arrived at the Clovelly café.

'Sorry I'm late,' I said, sitting down.

'No worries. Max has been keeping me busy.'

Jodie is my oldest friend. We grew up on the same street, went to the same high school and currently live only a few blocks away from each other. A year older and as smart as a chemical engineer, I've always looked up to Jodes, admiring her for her ability to go after (and get) what she wants from life. For example, when she was single, she decided she wanted to find a partner and so she implemented a plan of action to find one. Ironically, she met her partner Matt on a dancefloor during a night out. But as the old saying goes, 'Luck is when preparation meets opportunity.'

'So, I haven't seen you in ages. How's your love life?' she asked while wiping Max's nose. I made a few whimpering sounds. 'That bad, huh?'

'It's not even bad. It's non-existent. Although I would rather have a non-existent love life than a dysfunctional one, so I guess that's an improvement.'

'Have you thought about online dating?'

'Sure I've *thought* about it,' I grimaced. 'But that's about as far as I get.'

'You know, it doesn't carry the stigma it used to. Nowadays *everyone* is online.'

I took a sip of my coffee. 'It's not that I have anything against it. It just such an ... unromantic way of finding love.'

Jodie laughed. 'Have you read *The Rosie Project*? Perhaps that's the way you need to approach it.'

'I love that book,' I said, chuckling, and remembering how I had the same thought. It's a novel by Graeme Simsion about a socially challenged genetics professor called Don who's determined to find himself an 'appropriate' wife by having potential female candidates complete a questionnaire. He calls it his 'Wife Project'. As the questionnaire continues to alienate potential partners, Don meets Rosie, whom he quickly eliminates as an unsuitable partner as per his impossible criteria, but to whom he finds himself inexplicably drawn. 'Actually, I'm exploring other options.'

'Like what? An introduction agency?' Jodie seemed excited.

I shook my head. 'A fertility specialist,' I whispered even though we were the only ones in the café.

'To freeze your eggs?'

'To talk about my options. Freezing eggs is one option. Although a girlfriend did point out that I haven't exactly given one hundred per cent to exploring the dating option yet.'

'She's right,' Jodie said. 'You haven't, but if you want to have kids you can't waste time either. Keep in mind it's *hard work.* I don't know how single mothers do it.' She glanced at her son. 'As much as I love him, I don't have any time for myself, the house is always a mess and I feel like I'm rushing everywhere. I know that Matt and I should spend more time together but I'm always so exhausted.'

'Yeah, I'm not sure if it's what I want to do yet. I'm just going to have a chat.'

'It can't hurt. I think it's a smart thing to do.'

We talked for a little longer before we both had to get going. On the way home I thought more about our conversation. I'd never been sure whether I wanted kids, but nor did I want to find myself in my early forties, longing to be a mother and wishing I'd done something earlier. As Jodie said, being a parent is hard work and, as rewarding as that is, it's something you have to be committed to. Now that I'm discovering what that actually means, I'm even more aware of the importance of choosing your commitments carefully. And there's no greater commitment than bringing a child into the world.

I trudged back up the hill to my apartment, eager to start writing. Yet once I was back at my desk, the sound of drilling returned, piercing the air – along with my concentration. I pulled out my phone and typed the word 'drill' into my dream dictionary app.

Consulting a dream dictionary to help understand certain real life situations, in particular, the reoccurring ones, is something I've been doing for years. For a while I was witnessing a lot of car crashes while driving. My friend Astrid has a unique understanding of the supernatural, so one day after seeing yet another crash, I called her for advice.

'I don't know what's going on,' I said. 'I'm starting to freak out. I'm worried that it's some kind of sign.'

'There's nothing to worry about,' said Astrid confidently. 'It's just your subconscious working through your fears.'

'What do you mean?'

At the time I was days away from the launch of my first book. Even though it was a long-held dream, the reality was proving far less enjoyable. I was anxious about making something so personal public and, as the launch drew closer, my anxiety intensified.

'You're about to publish a book for the first time,' Astrid told me. 'It's a big deal. You've put your heart and soul into it and now you're putting it out there for people to judge and criticise you. It's a risk and it's out of your control.'

'Wow! That's amazing. How do you know all that?'

'I didn't. It just came to me. What you're seeing in your reality is an out-picturing of your inner reality. Right now, you're feeling out of control, so this is going to manifest into these pictures and visions. The car crash is a visual symbol for feelings that are buried so deep you wouldn't know they were there unless something brought them to your attention. If an image is flashing repeatedly in front of you, like a car crash, it's because you haven't acknowledged the underlying cause.'

'So what am I supposed to do?'

'Nothing. You've already done it just by having this conversation. You now know why you've been seeing them. My bet is that you won't see any more. Once you become aware of why an issue keeps showing up, that's when it dissolves, and it usually happens very quickly, if not instantly.'

Astrid was right. I didn't see another car crash and I recognised what was really going on. I *had* been feeling out of control about the release of my book and once I acknowledged this, the outer symbols dissolved.

That conversation showed me a new way of observing and interacting with the world. I began to see life as more like a dream, rather than a hard and fixed physical reality. There are layers to life, and there's more to it than meets the eye. Much more. What's in front of me isn't always the full story, yet it's up to me whether I want to know the full story. Life is a conversation with the Universe, which is always communicating with us through signs and symbols, situations and events. It made sense to consult a dream dictionary. Waking up in the morning isn't the end of the dream. It's a continuation.

The drilling is another example of reality trying to get my attention. If it wasn't for that relentless noise, I might not have noticed or cared. Yet it has my attention so I figure the Universe is trying to tell me something. According to the dream dictionary, seeing or hearing a drill means 'you are headed toward a new direction. You are opening yourself up to new experiences and insights'. For such an unpleasant noise, this was an uplifting message. Interestingly, ten minutes later, the drilling stopped and I was able to write in peace.

—

I'm a few hundred words short of my quota when I realise it's time to leave to meet Grace. But when I punch the address of the theatre into the car's GPS, I find the theatre is closer than I expected. I could run back inside and finish my words but just as I'm about to jump back out of the car, I have another thought.

Keep moving forward in the direction you're going. Trust life. There's a reason.

It's 5.29 pm when I walk through the foyer of the Seymour Centre. The theatre is devoid of human life other than a young man behind the snack counter stocking the fridge. I have half an hour to kill before meeting Grace so I figure I'll grab something to eat.

'Are you open?' I say, approaching the counter.

The young man spins around. 'Sure am. What can I get you?'

'I'll have a shiraz. And one of those.' I point to a bag of Maltesers, which was not part of my dinner plan.

The foyer's glass doors slide open and in walks Grace, looking elegant with a colourful shawl draped around her shoulders. 'You're early too!' I say, shocked by the synchronicity.

'There was no traffic. It was weird. It took me half the time to get here. Why are you here so early?'

'Just extraordinarily well-organised.'

'Ha!' says Grace. She orders a chardonnay.

As we wander over to an empty table we hear a female voice call out from behind: 'Hi girls!' I turn around to see a woman skipping through the empty foyer towards us. It's Vita, a friend of Grace's, and the writer of the play we're seeing tonight. I met Vita once several years ago, and she greets us both with a kiss and a hug that contains slightly more grip than normal.

'Oh my God,' she says. 'I'm *so* nervous. Someone please remind me why I keep putting myself through this. I feel so out of control right now and I hate it.'

I shake my head with laughter, knowing only too well what she's talking about. 'You're doing it because you're a writer, and this is what writers do.'

Vita closes her eyes and takes a deep breath. 'Keep going,' she says.

'You're doing it because you love it and you've written something great that everyone here, or everyone that soon will be here, is going to enjoy and find meaning in. But most importantly, you're doing it because you're good at it and this is your gift.'

She opens one eye and looks in my direction. Then she opens the other eye. All of a sudden she jerks forward and grabs hold of my thighs. 'I *loved* your book, Hedley. Have you written a follow-up? I want to know what happens next.'

Vita's talking about *Finding Paris: An Unusual Love Story*, the book I published two years earlier. 'I did but I decided not to publish it.'

'Why not? You have to.'

'I couldn't get it to work. I spent a year and a lot of money on it but in the end, I had to let it go. I haven't written anything since.'

'What?' Vita's eyes widen. 'But you have to keep writing. You *must*. What was it you just said? Something about this being your gift?'

'Thank you,' I say with a smile. 'That's kind of you.'

'I'm not trying to be kind; I'm being honest. If you want my advice – and I'm aware you probably don't – you *have* to keep writing. You *have* to keep telling stories. You're a writer, Hedley. That's what you do. That's what we do. That's what I'm doing.'

'Hedley's on a creative pilgrimage,' Grace says. 'She's writing two thousand words a day for the next thirty-one days.'

'I ... *love* ... that!' Vita cries. 'Go you! Are you going to publish it? I hope so. That's something I need to do. Oh God, I can't believe I'm doing this. Did I mention that I'm nervous?'

While I'm grateful I'm not in Vita's shoes, she's right. This is what writers do. This is what every artist does. We put ourselves in vulnerable positions every time we put our art in front of others. It's nerve-racking. But we do it anyway. The rewards end up outweighing the nerves. Most of the time, anyway.

I'm grateful that I listened to that inner wisdom earlier, nudging me to keep moving forward. Had I not trusted myself I wouldn't have had this extra half-hour or this extra magical conversation and time with my friends. Sometimes the option that doesn't make sense is the right one.

Insight of the Day

Commitment sometimes means inconvenience. To make a commitment to something means there is going to be a time when you're not going to feel like doing it. Do it anyway.

Day 6

No missed opportunities

Sleep is officially over. While the drilling might have stopped, it's been replaced by hammering. I roll over and grab my phone to consult the dream dictionary. By understanding the underlying meaning, I can potentially make it stop. Hammering symbolises 'determination and drive in pursuing your goals'. Okay, I agree with this. The hammering continues. I guess not everything has some profound meaning. I take it instead as a sign it's time to get up.

I push back the covers and reluctantly get out of bed. I'm still wrestling with the inconvenience of my commitment, unable to stop thinking about the remaining twenty-five days. Twenty-five days is a long time, and two thousand words are a lot of words. Combine these two facts and I'm left with an overwhelming feeling that this is all very inconvenient. But I can't give up. Again, this is inconvenient.

One day at a time, I remind myself. *One day at a time.*

Out the door and into the morning cold, I walk briskly towards the cemetery while trying to get warm. A couple of older men are pressed up against the metal fence, gazing out across the dark ocean. I stop and look in the same direction. A hundred metres or so offshore, a wall of white water rises along with a shiny black hump before disappearing again beneath the surface. It's a whale. A few seconds later there's another one, and another.

Whale: *A whale represents your intuition and awareness. You are in tune with your sense of spirituality. Alternatively, a whale symbolises a relationship or business project that may be too big to handle. You are feeling overwhelmed. It may also be a pun on 'wailing' and a desire to cry out about something.*

It's the last sentence that has me nodding. This is exactly how I'm feeling about this challenge. I'm scared I'm not going to follow through on my commitment. I'm scared what will happen if I don't. This fear has been here since I began the challenge, nestling itself into my guts and gripping my thoughts. The feeling is now heightened by the realisation that writing two thousand words a day is harder than I expected. I feel like jumping up and down and stamping my feet and having a great, loud wail.

But watching the huge creatures playing in the water has a surprisingly calming effect. Recognising how I'm feeling has allowed those feelings to dissipate. My neck and shoulders start to relax while the knot in my stomach loosens. I begin to breathe more slowly and deeply.

Heading back down the hill towards Earl's, I spot Brett in the distance, running from the opposite direction. His dogs, Buster and Rupert, trot alongside him. 'Brett!' I call when he's within earshot.

'Hey!' he says and waves, slowing down. 'How are you?'

'Great. I'm just on my way back from Clovelly. How far did you run?'

'To North Bondi and back.'

'Good on you.' I'm impressed.

'Not really. I'm supposed to be doing the City2Surf this year but at this rate I don't think I'm going to be fit enough. Hey, you should do it with us.'

'Ha,' I say, chuckling at the suggestion. 'I'm busy washing my hair that day.'

There are some commitments I simply have no interest in making and running around the city on a Sunday morning is one of them. It feels good to acknowledge this. Interestingly, knowing how capable I am of *not* committing to something is uplifting. We need to recognise when we do something well and I am good at *not* committing to a whole range of things, not only long-distance running. I'm not committed to learning Latin or playing the violin or becoming a chess champion. I'm not committed to line-dancing, playing croquet, calligraphy or video games. I'm not committed to doing any of these things, and it's liberating. Suddenly I have all this extra energy I can invest in those things I *am* committed to, like writing.

My phone beeps. 'Hang on,' I say. It's Boris, my Russian chiropractor, wondering where I am. 'Oh shit! Got to go.' I say a quick goodbye before turning towards home. Racing up the hill to my car, I wonder how I could forget my appointment with Boris when I've spent this entire week exploring the topic of commitment. While focused on everything I'm *not* committed to, I'm clearly still struggling with the 'follow through' aspect of what I *am* committed to. This isn't the first time I've almost missed my appointment with Boris. It might be due to a lack of a daily and consistent routine.

In the past when I've forgotten an appointment and received the text or phone call asking where I am, I would apologise profusely while accepting the fact I've missed my appointment, along with the financial consequences of having done so. I wouldn't even bother to show up. But this week it's different. Even though it's going to take half an hour just to get there, I made a commitment. I said I'd be there.

On the faster-than-normal drive over, I think about how this is an opportunity to redefine how I want to show up in the world. And that isn't someone who says one thing only to turn around and do the other, even if it's due to an undisciplined mind. I want to be someone who follows through. The kind of person who makes up their mind about doing something and then sticks to it, even if that means getting to an appointment late.

By the time I crash through Boris's door, I'm twenty-five minutes late, yet I feel as if I've got my money's worth. Boris hasn't laid a hand on me, but something inside feels as if it's been adjusted and I tell him so. He seems to understand what I'm talking about, almost as if he's had some hand in it (pardon the pun). This creative pilgrimage isn't just about writing two thousand words a day. It's about shaping and sharpening myself into the kind of person I want to be.

There are only five minutes left of my allotted time, and Boris taps the table, instructing me to get on it. He flicks his hand, hurrying me up. I crawl onto the bed, burying my face in the hole and closing my eyes. 'Look,' he says and I wait for him to begin one of his many rambling stories. 'Look!' he says again and I open my eyes. There's an iPad on the floor. On the screen is a photograph of a giant brown bear with her little cub sitting next to her.

'Why are you showing me this?' I ask.

Boris flicks the screen to the right, revealing the next picture. It's a photo of the same bear picking up the cub in her mouth. She looks as if she's about to launch the cub into the air. The expression on the little bear's face is one of shock and fear. Boris flicks the screen again. The next photo is of the cub sitting a couple of metres from his mother, looking hurt and confused. The next picture is the mother bear hugging her cub close to her.

'Okay ...' I say, not sure why Boris is showing me pictures of a bear flinging her cub around like a Frisbee. Boris does go off on random tangents at times.

'Mother teaching cub a lesson,' he says.

I get it. Life is a teacher and sometimes she gives us lessons that are uncomfortable but which inevitably push us into more powerful versions of ourselves. Sometimes these lessons are repeated until we get the point. I get the point, thinking back to all the times I've missed appointments only to offer a weak apology before moving on without a second's thought. An apology without some change in behaviour, however, is just empty words. There's no commitment. And uttering empty words on a regular basis is like running a bath without putting the plug in. It drains our energy and power. Every time I make a commitment and break it without taking action to correct it, I'm wasting energy. This is why it never feels good.

Doing what we say we are going to do is an act of self-love. It's a demonstration of respect both for ourselves and for others. But until we can truly commit to ourselves, I'm starting to understand, we can't commit to others. And committing to a creative calling is perhaps one of the greatest commitments we can make.

As I near the end of the first week of this creative pilgrimage, I realise I have not been committed to the craft of writing. Instead, I've been a dabbler, writing a little bit here and a little bit there. There's nothing wrong with being a dabbler, but I'm not here to dabble. I'm here to be the best version of myself, and I can't be that without making a commitment to creativity. And to be committed to creativity means keeping the pen moving even when I don't feel like it. *Especially* when I don't feel like it.

There will be times when we make up our minds about something and stick to it, only to muck it up anyway. This is where self-forgiveness is useful. As enlightening as these last few days have been, I'm sure that in the future I will still make commitments that I either break, forget about or just give up on. Although hopefully after this week, this number will be greatly reduced.

Insight of the Day

Know what you're committed to. Know what you're not committed to. Change everything you're *not* committed to and then invest that energy into everything you *are* committed to. Also, check your schedule at the beginning of the day. There's no need to make life difficult for yourself.

Day 7

The other 'F' word

I dreamt of frogs last night. Lots of them. Slimy, bouncing frogs. Some were so small, they were almost invisible. I couldn't see all of them, but I knew they were frogs. They were climbing and jumping all over me while I slapped and flapped my hands and arms about.

I consult the dream dictionary.

Frogs: *To see leaping frogs indicates your lack of commitment. You have a tendency to jump from one thing to another.*

This can't be right. What about this whole last week which I've spent reflecting on the topic of commitment and turning my relationship with it upside down? And let's not forget the seven days of written evidence. I could have given up on this project at least 129 times by now, but I didn't. So what are the frogs going on about?

My phone pings. An appointment reminder flashes up on the screen.

What? Not again!

Yes again. I've forgotten another appointment, this time to test-drive a new car. Perhaps the frogs have a point.

I shower and get dressed. Then I'm suddenly struck by a thought: *I don't actually want a new car.*

A few weeks back, I called the car dealership to check the status of the lease on my current car. Somehow during the conversation, the salesman launched into a passionate description of the new model. Admittedly, it sounded fantastic, even though I'm not in the market or the financial position to buy a new car. He offered to take me for a test drive. 'Obviously, there's no obligation,' he said in his confident, I'm-selling-you-but-you-don't-yet-know-it voice. I agreed on the basis that 'it can't hurt'. It's just a test drive. It's not like I'm going to buy it, even though I bought my current car because of another innocent test drive.

So, why was I rushing to test drive a car I don't need or want?

This has everything to do with what the car salesman is committed to, which is selling cars, and nothing to do with what I'm committed to, which has nothing to do with buying one. This is another valuable lesson: if we aren't clear about our commitments, we run the risk of being blind-sided by other people's, becoming unsuspecting pawns in their quest to meet their needs. In this case, the car salesman was and is so clearly committed to selling cars, his agenda beat my more wishy-washy one. As a result, I could have ended up with a gorgeous new car. *Wait. Hang on. How is this not okay?*

I call the salesman and leave a message, telling him I won't be coming in for a test drive. As much as I would love to buy a new car, I'm not in the position to do so. I feel instantly better.

With a spare hour to kill, I text Anna to see if she wants to meet for a coffee at Smith's. She agrees, and half an hour later we're slipping into one of the café's empty booths.

'How are your projects going?' I ask. Anna has been juggling a number of different clients, some more difficult and demanding than others.

'Well, actually,' she says, 'there's lots happening. I've decided to hire an assistant.'

'That's great news. What will they do?'

'Right now I'm drowning in paperwork so they'll take over most of the admin. I can't do it all. The whole reason I became an interior designer was that I love designing. If I could just spend a few more hours a week drawing, I'd be so much happier.'

'That sounds worth it then. Actually, that's what I'm writing about at the moment.'

'Hey, that's right. How's the challenge going?'

A surge of emotion rises unexpectedly. My eyes moisten and tears threaten to unleash themselves without any consideration of the fact that I'm in public. Anna's expression changes to concern. 'What's up?' she asks.

I shake my head, looking up and attempting to drain the water back into my eyes. 'I don't know.'

The tears begin their descent down my face which is not how I wanted this moment to play out. I grab a napkin just as Hendrix appears with our coffees. Noticing the emotional moment unfolding, he sets the coffees down and prances back to the kitchen without a word.

'I'm scared,' I say, grabbing the sleeve of my cardigan with my teeth.

'Of what? You're going so well.'

'Of everything. I've given up on so many things; I'm scared I'll give up on this too. What will I do if I can't even get through thirty-one days of doing the only thing I've ever wanted to do? And what about money? I can't afford to keep writing just for the hell of it, which is what it feels like I'm doing. I'm scared I'm going to fall back into that dark place again.'

Anna smiles and touches my arm. 'It's going to be okay. You're not going to give up because this is who you are. And even if you did, it wouldn't matter. You'll be okay because you *are* okay. If you're worried about money, you could always find a job you hate that only pays you a fifth of what you're worth. But I think you should just keep doing what you're doing and have a little more faith in yourself. Things have a way of working themselves out if you let them.'

I nod, grateful for the reassurance.

'Everything *is* working out,' Anna says. 'Right now, you've got money in the bank and that's all you need to know for the moment. You're doing what you're meant to do. Just keep writing.'

'Really?' I say, still unconvinced.

'I promise,' she says. 'It's not easy walking to the beat of your own drum. Sometimes you just have to block out anyone or anything that doesn't support what you're doing.'

'Thanks. I needed to hear that.'

'We all need to hear it now and then.'

The tension in my body melts like a block of ice on a hot day. This is the first step in rebuilding my life and putting it back together in a way that is aligned with what feels good and right. I will always write whether I make a cent from it or not. Do what you love and the money will follow, as my dad would always say, but don't do it just for the money. That's the fastest route to writer's block. I just have to trust. Start with creativity and let the rest of the path reveal itself from there.

—

Back in front of my computer, instead of starting my two thousand words, I click open the manuscript I had been working on but which I cast to the side after completing the eleventh draft and becoming bored with it. Eleven drafts will sometimes have that effect. It's going to be tough earning a living as a writer if I'm not prepared to finish what I started just because I got bored. There are always going to be periods when something is boring and monotonous. This is not a reason to stop and give up, especially if it's something you love.

The manuscript is called *Creative Keynote: 7 Keys to Public Speaking Artistry for Creative Professionals*. It's based on my work as a public speaking coach. It's intended to help people; in particular, creative professionals, overcome their fear of public speaking, as well as promote my work as a public speaking coach. It would, therefore, be useful to finish it. After all, I'd like to make a living from writing and this requires commitment.

Maybe this is what the frogs were trying to tell me?

Creative Keynote is an example of the creative fling mentality. With the excitement of writing the first few drafts over, the book became a series of tedious To Do items, including editing, more editing, proofreading, typesetting and everything else that goes with transforming a manuscript into a published book. Getting a manuscript ready for publication can often take just as long as the writing, if not longer. I put *Creative Keynote* to the side around the time when the real work began.

It's important to follow through on the commitments I've made by finishing what I've already set out to do. This is instead of hunting for the next big idea and creative high. Finishing what I started might help ward off unexpected emotional breakdowns in the middle of cafés. Not only that: finishing something creates the space for something else. Commitment is not just following through on the projects you've started, but following through on the ones you've almost finished as well.

To be an artist, especially a professional one, you have to work hard and be persistent. Creativity is not flighty and non-committal.

It's not moody and indecisive. Creativity doesn't wake up and think 'I don't feel like being creative today'. Creativity is what it's always been. It's the objective constant. Human beings are the ones who wake up and avert our attention from what is a natural state of being. Creativity is our natural state because we are a product of creation. In fact, human beings are one of the most magnificent creations in the history of the Universe. Creativity isn't just in our blood; it *is* our blood.

In *Wild*, Cheryl Strayed wrote about the monotony, the intense boredom, the frustration, the exhaustion and other undesirable realities of her journey. These realities, I'm realising, are part of every creative journey, particularly the ones that matter the most. Committing to our creative callings requires facing our humanness. That is our flaws and frailties and habits of distraction. Whether you're walking across the country, directing a movie, setting up a business or writing a book, there's no getting around the fact that it's going to get hard and uncomfortable. At some point, it'll feel like the last thing you want to be doing. Commitment is doing it anyway because you said you would.

Over the next few hours, I comb through the first chapter of *Creative Keynote*, deleting and rewriting, moulding and shaping. It's slow and laborious work. After four hours or so, I've done four pages. For a manuscript that's over two hundred pages long, there's a long way to go. Yet I don't suddenly become distracted and start looking for something else to do. Instead, I stand up and stretch, take a long drink of water and then sit down and get back to work.

Thank you, frogs.

Insight of the Day

Be aware of anything that could potentially distract you from doing what you've committed to, especially other people's commitments. There are going to be times when what you're doing is boring and monotonous. These are not the times to give up. Rather, these are the times to strengthen your commitment.

Part II - Ambition

From Latin *ambitionem* (nominative *ambito*) 'a going around'.

A strong desire to do or achieve something.

Day 8

The long way around

It's Saturday morning and I'd prefer to be asleep but I'm not. Nor am I likely to be. There's a conversation going on outside my bedroom window between my neighbour and a man who, I notice, has an attractive, almost mesmerising voice. Unfortunately, not mesmerising enough to put me back to sleep. Clear and pronounced with the right combination of articulation and casual twang, it's a voice that would suit a country radio station or a beer commercial. I listen for a while before rolling over and placing a pillow over my head.

If there's one activity I'm committed to it's sleeping, and it's something I've become good at. An ex once nicknamed me 'the log' for my capacity to sleep through anything, including a violent case of food poisoning he experienced in the middle of the night. The bond I've developed with sleeping is almost unbreakable, even though I have tried to break it countless times.

As much as I love sleeping, however, there's a part of me that also yearns to rise with the sun. There's something powerful and sacred about waking early, even if I'm rarely awake to experience it. On the few occasions when I do start the day earlier and more consciously, it undoubtedly unfolds more effortlessly and naturally, like turning the page of a pop-up book.

Unfortunately, this early, conscious start to the day is the exception. I usually prefer to stay wrapped in unconsciousness for as long as possible. The more I yearn to rise earlier, the longer I sleep. A good night's sleep is healthy but a good night's sleep plus a few more hours of dozing isn't. I suspect my sleeping habits are doing me more harm than good. They need to change, but I'm not sure how. It feels impossible.

Excessive sleeping is an avoidance tactic I employed wholeheartedly after I finished my last book. After a year of working on it, I just couldn't get it right and I made the decision not to publish it. The experience left me feeling deflated, and I began to lose enthusiasm for everything, including writing. I started staying in bed longer and getting up later while telling myself, 'I need the rest.' After all, it's tiring writing a book that you don't feel is very good. Sleep became a friendly shoulder upon which I rested my head.

I've since fallen into an unhealthy habit. It's been months since I've set my alarm, leaving the job to my natural body rhythms, which are tuned to the rhythms of sleep. When a sliver of light slices through a crack in the curtain, I begin the slow process of coming to terms with the fact that my night of blissful unconsciousness is over and real life has begun once more. This requires an adjustment period involving at least another hour. By the time I do manage to drag myself out from under the covers, new apps have been developed, societies have been overthrown, and world records have been broken.

Sleeping in, I've come to realise, isn't conducive to creative output. And creative output is something I'd like to increase. What to do? Get up earlier would be the obvious answer but this is easier said than done. Much easier. The moment I even start contemplating rising earlier, the more exhausted I start to feel. In a recent attempt to inspire myself, I wrote the words of a poem, *The Breeze at Dawn* by the thirteenth-century Sufi poet, Rumi, on a piece of paper and stuck it next to my bed:

The breeze at dawn has secrets to tell you.
Don't go back to sleep.
You must ask for what you really want.
Don't go back to sleep.
People are going back and forth across the doorsill
Where the two worlds touch.
The door is round and open.
Don't go back to sleep.

I'd hoped 'the breeze at dawn' and its promise of secrets would help pull me out from under the covers. All it did was highlight just how attached to staying under them I've become, especially on Saturday mornings when the idea of sharing it with newspaper-reading couples and families en route to Saturday morning sport doesn't exactly appeal.

Hauling myself out of bed and into the late morning, I grab a takeaway coffee and head towards the calming surrounds of Centennial Park. I think I'll sit under one of the large fig trees, away from the weekend crowds. I drive around the park several times in search of the perfect fig tree yet I can't seem to make a decision.

Parking the car, I think I'll search on foot, but I just find myself walking around in circles. I have no idea what I'm doing or where I'm going.

Henri is tucked safely into the side pocket of my pants, pressing up against my leg along with the pressure of two thousand words still waiting to be written. I'm wondering if the theme for this week is going to reveal itself and when this might be.

My phone pings and I'm grateful for the distraction. It's a text from Mum, saying that my book has arrived. I don't know what she's talking about but I'm glad to now have something to do with my Saturday morning. Perhaps this book can offer some inspiration.

Entering the empty kitchen at my mum's, I spy the book buried among the morning newspapers on the dining table. *Daily Rituals: How Great Minds Make Time, Find Inspiration, and Get to Work* by Mason Currey. I pick it up and flop onto the lounge in the sunroom as the midday sun streams in through the skylight above. On the first page is a profile on the artist W.H. Auden. The first line reads: 'Routine, in an intelligent man, is a sign of ambition.'

The word 'ambition' jumps off the page. Something about it feels familiar and I say the line out loud.

Routine. A sign of ambition.

A sign of ambition.

Ambition.

I can't grasp why it's familiar yet it feels significant. I let the word roll around in my mind for a few moments and then ...

That's it!

Ambition was the second word I saw painted in black along the path. *Commitment. Ambition. Determination. Sacrifice. Courage.* Ambition is the theme for the second week of this pilgrimage. It's not a word that's ever resonated with me. It seems to suggest pushing, forcing, manipulating and treading over others in pursuit of one's agenda. It's the only word out of all the words on the path I resisted. Yet perhaps there's more to it than I'm aware of. Perhaps it's time to develop a healthier, positive relationship with ambition. Investigating further, I look up the original definition.

Ambition: *A strong desire to do or achieve something.*

It comes from the Latin, *ambire*, which means to 'go around', something I was doing a lot of a couple of hours ago. I sense there's more to discover about ambition, in particular the role routine plays. If routine is a quality of ambition then I have a lot to learn. I've never been a fan of routine. It's always been something of a party pooper, a killer of creative fun and freedom, so why would I want to invite such a concept into my life? Unfortunately, this way of thinking isn't compatible with getting things done. Productivity works best when there's some kind of plan, structure or schedule. This might explain my lack of creative output in recent years. Not to mention the aimless circles I've been wandering around in recently.

Despite my resistance to routine, there was one time when I consciously chose to engage in one on a daily basis. While writing *Finding Paris*, I developed and, rather surprisingly, stuck to a daily schedule that enabled me to finish the manuscript in six months. It helped that I was brimming with enthusiasm and eagerness, but this approach was in stark contrast to the one I took with my first book, which took three long and torturous years of sporadic writing intermingled with long stretches of avoidance and procrastination.

When it came time to write *Finding Paris*, however, I decided to do it differently, as in *routinely*. I would be at my desk at ten o'clock each weekday morning, and there I would remain until five in the afternoon. I blocked out the time in my diary, refusing to schedule appointments within my allocated writing time. After six months, I had the first draft of a manuscript along with a profound sense of accomplishment, a feat that wouldn't have been possible without sticking to a daily routine.

This experience showed that rather than stifling creativity, a daily regime can provide a place for it to roam and run free. Structure and routine offered a space so the story could come to life. It didn't matter whether I felt like writing or not, or even whether the writing was any good. My goal was to show up every day and write until the job was done. My desire to write *Finding Paris* was greater than my resistance to structure and routine. Interestingly, it was one of the most enjoyable creative experiences I've had to date. A correlation, perhaps?

—

Later that afternoon, I take a walk around the cliffs to my favourite bench overlooking Clovelly Beach. By the time I arrive the sun has already dropped below the ocean, along with the temperature, leaving the sky awash with a stunning array of watercolour pinks and purples and blues. Other than a couple of young guys huddled together on the grassy slope nearby, the place is quiet. One is strumming on a guitar while the other is playing a ukulele. They're absorbed in the melody they're creating. It's inspiring. Despite the cold, these guys are making their music, singing their song. They are engaged with creativity, having shown up when it might have been easier to stay at home.

Perhaps this is what ambition looks like.

Insight of the Day

Having ambition means having a strong desire to do something, to achieve something. This doesn't mean walking over people in order to make it happen. Instead, it can be an invitation to make a plan, create a daily routine and stick to it.

Day 9

Taking a stand

'Could we stop by the mall on the way home and check out Fine & Sonny?' asks Anna as we hop into the car. 'They've just opened a boutique and I've been wanting to have a look.'

I'd also heard of the new clothing brand which had just opened their first store in Bondi Junction and was quickly gaining a cult following, but had resisted stopping for a sticky-beak. I didn't need to be tempting myself with unnecessary 'must haves'.

'Sure. Just don't let me buy anything. I can't afford to be spending money on clothes right now, as beautiful as they might be.'

'Okay,' says Anna with a laugh. 'You don't have to buy anything but I can't promise that I won't.'

Anna and I have spent the last two hours having some photos done for our respective websites. Naturally, I decided to massacre the three monstrosities which had recently arrived on my face the night before, requiring a bottle of foundation and concealer to cover up. But we were in good hands and if anyone could make us look presentable, it was our young and talented photographer, Beth.

Both Anna and I have long admired Beth's work and when I found out she was coming to Sydney to stage an exhibition, I contacted her to ask if she would be willing to do a quick shoot. Watching her move around the spacious studio with confidence and ease made it clear we were working with not just an artist but a *professional.* Photography is as much Beth's passion as it is her job.

Beth is focused and committed to getting the most out of every shot, yet appears to do this without stress or tension. She's relaxed and self-assured without being arrogant. She takes pride in her work and I sense this comes more from within than the standards or expectations of others. She pushes herself to do and be better for no other reasons than her own. She's ambitious.

When Anna and I arrive at Fine & Sonny's crisp white store I realise it's going to be a much tougher task to keep my credit card inside my wallet. The beautifully designed clothes, draped elegantly on their wooden hangers, are begging to be touched, tried on and ultimately bought. Glancing around the shop, I spy at least four items I'm in urgent need of. Anna is already heading towards the architecturally appealing changing rooms with a pile of clothes over one arm. It's safer to take a seat at the table in the centre where the racks remain out of reach.

'How are you today?' asks an assistant, all fresh-faced and smiling.

'Well, thanks,' I say, my gaze still fixed on the black slip dress hanging on the mannequin in the window.

'Would you like to try it on?'

I shake my head. 'No, thanks. I promised myself that I wasn't going to buy anything, which is probably not what you want to hear. I'll just sit here and wait for my friend if that's okay.'

'Sure, no problem. Sit back and relax.'

Anna emerges from the dressing room in a gorgeous tan cashmere overthrow.

'Oh God,' I say. 'Go away. It's so gorgeous I can't look. You're making this very difficult.'

'You like?' she asks, taking another spin before disappearing back behind the curtains. I notice a flyer in the middle of the table. As it's the only item in the store that doesn't have a price tag on it, I lean over to pick it up.

NOTHING WORKS WITHOUT INTEGRITY

It's a company motto. The quote, by business theorist Chris Argyris, continues: 'People are mostly unaware that they have not kept their word. All they see is the "reason", rationalisation or excuse for not keeping their word. In fact, people systematically deceive themselves about who they have been and what they have done.'

The words are especially poignant. I often tell myself stories about why I haven't been writing, and why I don't or can't write every day. Self-deception is a skill, one I employ often when it comes to creative practice. Even when I know how important it is to sit down and write, I'll still manage to come up with a bunch of reasons why now is not the right time.

'Great, isn't it?'

The assistant has noticed my interest.

'It sure is,' I say. 'I love this message.'

'Fine & Sonny isn't one of those companies that just says it but doesn't mean it. They take an interest in who we are as individuals and what we're about. Each morning we all have to set two intentions: a personal one as well as a professional one. They want to help us achieve whatever it is we want to achieve so that we're happy not just when we come to work but in all areas of our lives.'

'That's really cool. So, what's one of your intentions?'

'Well, I used to love yoga and then I got into a relationship and

I just stopped going. The relationship took over my life. When we broke up I decided I wanted to get back into yoga. I remembered how good I felt, so I set an intention to do a yoga class every morning which meant setting the alarm for five ...'

'*Five?*' I say, suddenly nervous about where this conversation is heading.

She chuckles. 'I know it's really early. In the beginning it was hard, but I found that I was so much more productive. Having that time to myself to meditate and make a cup of tea set me up to have a much better and happier day.'

'You know, I've been thinking about getting up earlier for exactly that reason.'

'You should,' says the girl. 'Seriously, you'll feel so much better. It's hard to start with but once you're up, it's absolutely worth it.'

I pause, thinking about the suggestion. 'Maybe I could start by getting up at five-thirty?' Despite my loyalty to sleep, I do have a genuine desire to rise earlier, even though I'm not convinced it's possible.

The girl's expression morphs into excitement. 'Yes. I started getting up at five-thirty for a while. Once I knew I could do that, I made it five.'

'Okay, I'm doing it,' I say with an emphatic nod. 'I'm going to start getting up at five-thirty.'

I'm not at all confident with this declaration, especially since I was still comatose at nine this morning. Giving up an extra couple of hours of sleep is not going to be easy.

'Awesome,' the girl says. 'Now you're going to have to come back and report on how you're going.'

'Really?'

'Absolutely. You have to be accountable to someone. Otherwise, it's too easy to give up.'

'Right,' I say, nodding. 'So I'm really doing this.'

'You are *so* doing this.'

'What do you think?' says Anna, appearing from behind the white curtain, adorned in another long camel cardigan that looks as if it were made especially for her long, lithe frame.

'Okay, you're killing me now,' I say, laughing. 'It's stunning.'

'It's gorgeous,' says the shop assistant. 'That was definitely meant for you.'

'I'm getting it,' says Anna, turning around and flicking the curtain closed behind her once more.

And I'm getting up at five-thirty!

It's going to be a challenge. It's going to be a *challenging* challenge. Perhaps even an impossible one, but I'm determined to try. I want to come back to the store and tell the shop-assistant-slash-life-coach I've kept my word. I'm sure she's right about having someone to be accountable to. If she wasn't so forthcoming about reporting back, I'm not sure I could do it. It can be tough to change long-held habits. Sometimes we just need a little help, even if that help happens to be a shop assistant whom you've just met.

While Anna buys her new cardigan, the shop assistant turns her attention to another customer while I turn my attention back to the company's manifesto.

What you say you stand for: What you stand for, whether expressed in the form of a declaration made to one or more people, or even to yourself, as well as what you hold yourself out to others as standing for (formally declared or not), is a part of your word.

It's as if I'm in a conversation with the Universe and it's communicating with me through seemingly random yet perfectly orchestrated situations and people and places and strategically placed pieces of papers. This isn't the first time I've experienced this phenomenon, yet it's the first time I've experienced it on a daily basis. It could be because I'm paying closer attention to the world around me but it could also be because I'm writing every day. Either way, life is turning out to be a more magical and mysterious adventure as a result of this creative pilgrimage. It's the perfect motivation to want to start the day a few hours earlier.

Insight of the Day

Make the decision to be an artist. Get up earlier. Have integrity. Keep your word, even if it's just to yourself. Stand for something. Declare it. Engage in a conversation with the Universe. Listen. Learn to 'speak' the silent language.

Day 10

Easier said than done

This is going to be harder than I thought. As soon as I opened my eyes, I knew this was more than just a fling. I'm in love. Totally, madly and deeply. Although I'm not sure why I'm surprised. We've been spending a lot of time together, mostly in the bedroom, tangled up among the sheets, but also on the couch. You might say we're in a long-term relationship, yet it's more like a marriage. At least that's how it feels. I'm not just in a relationship with sleep; I'm married to it. Beautiful, dependable, irresistible sleep is my lifelong, loving and loyal partner.

We're childhood sweethearts. After all, I have been asleep for at least a quarter of my life, if not more. Did I think I could just wake up one morning and decide to get divorced? Did I think I could just end the relationship with the flick of a switch? That all of a sudden I could just bounce out of bed at five-thirty as if this were the most natural thing to do? As if I've been doing this my entire life? Did I really think it was going to be so easy? Well, apparently, I've been kidding myself.

I vaguely recall the sound of the angelic chimes ringing somewhere in the vicinity of my right ear. I don't remember grabbing my phone and throwing it across the room, even though this is what happened because this is where I found it when I woke again three hours later. By the time I finally entered the land of the living, the construction workers down the street were already sitting down for their morning tea break. Sleep had won again. I was disappointed, to say the least.

It was my genuine intention to rise early enough to catch the sunrise and begin my day on a positive, inspiring note. Last night, I even double-checked my alarm to make sure it was set to the correct time, placing it on the pillow where it would be sure to wake me with a fright in the morning. I even said the words out loud before falling asleep: 'Tomorrow I *choose* to get up at 5.30 am.' I wanted to remind myself that getting up early was a choice and therefore something I was capable of doing. I also wanted to inform my loving partner, sleep, that this was how it was going to be.

Unfortunately, this wasn't how it was. Sleep obviously isn't going to let me go that easily. Sleep, it seems, has a jealous streak. It's not like I want to end my relationship with sleep altogether. Just reduce it. It's clear we've been spending too much time together, and the relationship is beginning to encroach on my other relationships, in particular, the one with creativity. I want to devote more time to writing. This means sleeping less. Sleep has been the place I've long sought refuge in from my problems, along with doubt and insecurity. Whenever life became too hard, or I felt down or unsure of myself, I could always just climb into bed and go to sleep. Sleep would welcome me into its warm and nurturing arms, enveloping me in a blissful state of unconsciousness. This is partly why I swallowed those pills. I just wanted to go to sleep and stay there forever.

My relationship with sleep needs to change. It's become codependent, and this isn't healthy. Sleep doesn't want me to write. It wants me to keep sleeping. Writing, on the other hand, doesn't care either way. There's always tomorrow. Sleep doesn't see it like that. It will pull out all the moves to convince me to stay in bed or have a lie-down. *Just for five minutes*, sleep will whisper. But it's never just five minutes.

Sleep has an answer for everything, and it's very convincing. *C'mon, you know you don't want to get up. You're still tired. It's too early. You haven't had your eight hours yet. You haven't even had seven. You need your rest. The shop assistant doesn't know what she's talking about. She's probably lying. You're not a morning person. Just stay a little longer. You know you want to. Surely a few more minutes can't hurt? Five more minutes. Just five more minutes and then you can get up.*

Of course, sleep can't actually talk, which is probably part of the reason we've been together for so long. Instead, these messages come from my waking-that-just-wants-to-go-back-to-sleep mind, and unless I fix these thoughts, there's no hope of ever making that much-needed change.

—

My friend Rhett is sitting at one of the tables along the wall when I arrive at Earl's. It's after nine. Rhett is both an actor and a writer. He understands the challenges that come with living a creative life.

'What time do you get up?' I ask him, pulling out the empty chair opposite.

'Anywhere between five-thirty and six,' he says as if it's the most natural act in the world. 'Why?'

'I want to get up earlier so I can get more out of the day but it's impossible. When the alarm goes off, I have no control over my body. It's like it's programmed to sleep.'

Rhett thinks about this for a second. 'Maybe you're focusing too much on the getting up part.'

'What do you mean?'

'Well, rather than focusing on the getting up early, how about focusing on what you intend to do once you're up?'

I pause for a moment. 'That makes sense. I *am* focused on the getting up part and it's proving impossible. So you're saying don't focus on getting up and instead focus on what I'm going to do once I'm up?'

Rhett nods. 'Why do you want to get up early?'

'I want to do more with my day.'

'Like what?'

'I want to meditate, I want to go for a walk, I want to watch the sunrise. I especially want more time to write.'

'So then focus on all the reasons *why* you're getting up rather than the actual process of getting up. Focus on why not how.'

'Huh. I've never thought of it like that. Focus on why. I like it. I think that could work. Thanks.'

'You know what else you could do?' says Rhett. 'Have you thought about joining a community of writers? It might help to have a group of like-minded people to talk to about this stuff.'

'It's funny you say that. I was thinking about doing exactly that the other day. I found one through Meet Up. I'm going to check it out next week. Why don't you come with me?'

A look of horror crosses his face. 'There's no way I'm joining a writers' group.'

'Why not? It was your idea!'

'I never take my own advice. Writing groups are scary. I prefer introversion and solitude. But you should go. Really.'

I laugh. 'I'm going so if you change your mind let me know.' I check the time on my phone. 'Well, it's time to go.' I finish my coffee before pulling out some change and dropping it on the table.

'Where are you off to?' Rhett asks.

'I've got two thousand words to write and they're not going to write themselves, although sometimes I wish they would.'

Insight of the Day

It's a new day. If at first you fail, and there will be times when you will, start again. If you continue to fail, keep starting again. Be gentle with yourself. Focus on why you're doing something rather than how you're going to do it.

Day 11

Be kind to your craft

I pull back the wire and slip through the gap in the fence, climbing the cliff face to a nook overlooking the dark, cellophane-like ocean. With the sun yet to take the stage, the sky continues to brighten as if someone were slowly turning up the lights. Leaning back against the cold rock, I sit cross-legged, gazing towards the horizon which is aglow with the promise of a spectacular show. I take a long, slow, deep breath. I can hardly believe I'm here.

Not surprisingly, I almost didn't make it. When the angelic chimes of the alarm, which are not angelic at that time of the morning, began chiming, my body prepared to go into battle once more. Yet as I was preparing to cast the phone across the room, something happened. I had a thought: *Why don't I just get up?*

Of course! It was so simple. Why don't I just get up? I could forget the strategies and mind tricks. They didn't work anyway. I could just throw back the covers, swing my feet over the side of the bed and stand up. It didn't need to be dramatic. It didn't need to be a big deal; I could just get up and not think about it. It's better that I don't. Ever.

And so I did. I got up. Just like that. I perched up in bed in a state of shock.

It was just after five.

I took a few moments to inhale this new and unfamiliar world.

The silence was profound. Deafening almost. There were no muffled conversations outside the window, no creaking floorboards or footsteps overhead, no crying or overexcited children running up and down the hallways. There was no beep-beep-beeping of trucks reversing. No clanking and clinking of falling bottles. No intermittent drilling or sanding or banging. Just silence. Beautiful, perfect silence. Except for the occasional morning song of a bird and the secret whispers of the morning breeze.

Waiting on the cliffs for the first ray to reveal itself, I recall the last time I was up early enough to see a sunrise. It was back in January, in India. Anna and I had booked into an Ayurvedic resort in the southern town of Kerala. We had decided to start the year clean and cleansed. During our stay, we learnt that one of the most beautiful sights in India was sunrise over the Kumari Amman temple in Kanyakumari.

We organised a car and a driver to take us on the two-hour drive to Kanyakumari, the southernmost tip of the Indian subcontinent where three bodies of water – the Arabian Sea, the Bay of Bengal, and the Indian Ocean – meet. Pick-up time was scheduled for four-thirty in the morning, the only part of the adventure I wasn't looking forward to. In a rush to get dressed, I slipped into a pair of white shorts and T-shirt, my standard beach attire. The closer we got to Kanyakumari, the closer I came to realising this was no ordinary trip to the beach. With the morning still enveloped in darkness, people streamed onto the streets, appearing from everywhere. Soon our van was engulfed in a crowd of several hundred, all dressed in saris and shawls that respectfully covered bare skin. I looked down at my tiny white shorts and grimaced.

This was an event, and not a one-off event either. It happened every morning, thousands of people rising early and making the trek to the edge of the ocean to celebrate the arrival of the new day. Never in my life had I seen so many people in one place at the same time. They were *everywhere*. Some were waving flags while others were carrying their seventeen offspring on their shoulders. Everyone was chanting and singing. It was a celebration of epic proportions. It reminded me of Mardi Gras in Sydney, except with everyone wearing a lot more clothes. As far as I could see, my two bare legs were the only bare legs on display.

I've never prayed for the sun to hurry up and rise the way I did that morning. Feeling the thousands of pairs of dark, curious eyes fixed on me and my legs, I was desperate for the sun to rise so we could get back to the safety and warmth of the van. All I had to cover up was a scarf which I needed to keep wrapped around my bare shoulders to offset the wind that was whipping around the point of Kanyakumari. What was supposed to be a memorable experience of watching a sunrise turned into the memorable but far less enjoyable experience of being watched.

The sunrise in Kanyakumari is in sharp contrast to my current surrounds. Aside from a meditator and a young guy practising his breakdancing moves further up the cliff, I have the place to myself. I can enjoy and appreciate this spectacular miracle of life. This is the *why* Rhett was talking about yesterday. The beauty of the early morning is so wondrous it's worth pushing through the discomfort of getting up early. I now have the pleasure of watching the grey marshmallow clouds with their fat pink bellies brighten and change colour as the sun continues its climb towards the edge of the horizon.

This is *why* it's worth rising early. There are secrets in this moment. I close my eyes and listen.

A force compels me to pull out Henri. The words appear on the page in a single brushstroke.

There are no such things as 'shitty words'.

I contemplate the sentence, which has appeared without any planning or conscious thought. It seems to be in response to a phrase I've heard about the writing process. 'The first words are always the shittiest.' I notice this a lot when I talk about writing and every time, the phrase grates. Along with its cousin phrase, 'The first draft is always a shitty draft.'

I'm aware of the state of most first drafts, having written several of them myself, yet this saying has never sat well with me. Suddenly I understand why. The words themselves are not shitty. They're just words. And like all words, they have a purpose. In most cases, however, this purpose does not lie in the final draft of a manuscript. This doesn't make them bad or terrible or *shitty*. The first words give way for second and third words. In which case, we should be grateful they showed up at all. The first words are the first to show up and grace us with their presence. How can we judge these words as shitty because they happened to be the first on the scene?

Editing is a crucial and essential part of the writing process, and the first words are like the soldiers on the front line. They sacrifice themselves for the better, stronger words that follow. First words are not destined for fame and stardom and the bright light of a reader's bedside lamp. They're almost always the first to go. Without first words, there is no book. Rarely is the first draft ever the final draft. Even writing these first words now, I'm sure they won't end up being the ones you are reading now. These words have been changed, added, deleted, altered again, polished and moulded over many drafts. Without those first fearless words, this sentence, this paragraph, this chapter, this book, would never have been possible. We all have to start somewhere. Making art might be the only time when being first doesn't always mean the being the best.

It takes courage to strike that pure and perfect page or canvas for the first time. Like a painter slashing a white space with a burst of colour. First words or brush strokes or chords are our babies, and we need to love and care for them in the same way we love those final fully-developed ones.

I've never felt protective of my words before. Not like this. Perhaps it has something to do with having to come up with two thousand new ones every day. It's not easy. Every morning I wake feeling apprehensive and queasy, wondering if the words will arrive or if today will be the day when they finally run out. I've been secretly dreading the moment when I sit down with my notebook or computer, my fingers poised in position only for them to seize up, having discovered the well of inspiration has finally evaporated. I've never written so many words on a daily basis. Is it possible to run out of words to write?

So far they've continued to come and when they do I feel a sense of gratitude that grows stronger every day. Suddenly the sun peeks above the sharp line of the horizon, sending the sky into a blaze of brilliant orange. It's a stunning sight and it happens every single morning. I realise the words will keep coming as long as I keep showing up to write them. As the sun continues to rise, the creative spirit continues to create through us. Creativity is infinite. Life never stops evolving. Musicians will always come up with new and unique melodies, painters will always paint never-seen-before artworks and writers will always write new, untold stories. There is no shortage of light, and no shortage of words.

Knowing I no longer have to worry about running out of words or ideas, I move through the rest of the day with a newfound sense of ease and peace. As long as I'm showing up to do my part – sitting down to write – the rest will be taken care of. Creativity is a co-creative process. I'm not in this alone, none of us are. We don't have to know how everything is going to work out, only that it will.

—

That evening, I head over to Mum's for a home-cooked meal of sausages, mashed spuds and veggies. Over dinner, I fill her in on my plans to go to Melbourne for the Melbourne Writers Festival at the end of the month, a decision I made long before coming up with the idea for a creative pilgrimage. The timing couldn't be more perfect.

'Who's headlining the event?' asks Mum, carefully slicing a carrot into thin strips.

'Louis de Bernières.'

'He wrote *Captain Corelli's Mandolin* and *Red Dog*. Wonderful books.'

'I haven't read either of them. I don't think I've read any of his books.'

'You might want to if he's going to be speaking. He's a great writer. I think I've got a copy of *Red Dog* somewhere. Do you want me to have a look?'

'Sure, if you don't mind.'

I follow her into the study. An entire wall of shelf space is filled with more books than there is space to hold them. Having survived the many 'spring cleans' over the years, the books are piled on top of each other, squeezed into every available nook. Some of the titles are recent, but many of them are decades old. I spy an ancient copy of *The Joy of Sex*. 'You still have this?' I say, pulling the book out and showing Mum.

'It appears so. I had no idea.'

'Sure,' I say with a chuckle. 'I bet you didn't!'

My eyes fall on a skinny orange spine. 'Here it is,' I say, prying the little book out from between two bigger books. When I pull it out, it isn't *Red Dog* but another of Louis de Bernières's books: *Labels*. My father gave it to me many years ago.

'I don't think I have *Red Dog*, after all,' says Mum, still searching the shelves. 'I must have given it away in the last cull.'

But I was already flicking through the novella. 'Oh my God.'

'What is it?' asks Mum, climbing down the stepladder.

I hand her the book, showing the handwritten note and signature inscribed on the first page.

For Hedley

Louis de Bernières, 1998

'Well, isn't that amazing?' she says.

'I'd forgotten that Dad had it signed for me.'

'Some things are meant to be.'

On the drive home, I remember the sparkle in my father's eyes as he insisted I look inside the book. While I don't remember opening it or seeing my name there, I remember the excitement on his face. With the book resting on the front seat of the car beside me, it's like my father is sitting there too.

Insight of the Day

There are no shitty words, only the first words. They are the soldiers on the frontline of first drafts. Be grateful for them. Be kind to them. They show up knowing their fate. First words are rarely the last words. Creativity is infinite. The words will keep coming as long as you keep showing up to write them.

Day 12

Staying grounded

I may have spoken too soon about the whole 'there are no shitty words' thing. Sometime during the last seven hours, all that positivity and creative exuberance has evaporated. I have a faint memory of a sunrise and something about an infinite well of inspiration. As for those first words, I contemplate them with a sense of loathing. Somehow I have to get them on the page. Again. But I'm tired, no doubt from waking up so early yesterday.

My thoughts drift to coffee, as they tend to do first thing in the morning. Coffee has long been a daily pleasure and ritual, offering social connection and conversation, as well as a caffeine hit. I've made many friends over coffee and seeking it out each morning is one of my favourite parts of the day.

After I amble slowly down the hill to the café, Earl greets me with his usual smile and a high five from behind the counter.

'Long black?' he asks.

I nod, glancing around for familiar faces. There are none, so I slide into one of the booths and open Henri to an empty page. I stare at the emptiness for a long time.

No words spring to mind, not even the first, so-called brave and gallant ones. I turn my attention towards the ocean which proves a far more enticing view. Rhett, my actor/writer friend, strolls in, hands interlocked with a young, attractive brunette. He looks smitten, and I assume it's the girl he met on the set of a short film. He introduces her as 'Sophie' before floating off to a table at the back of the café where they merge into a single person. I turn my attention back to the ocean, wishing I had a lover as a distraction from the words I'm not writing. Not that I need another person to distract me. I'm doing an excellent job of that myself.

On days like this – when getting the words onto the page feels like having a tooth extracted – I know I absolutely *must* write. Writing when I don't want to or feel like it is when creative muscles are made. Plus, it strengthens my creative confidence and my commitment to the craft. I continue chewing on my pen and staring at the ocean while nodding my head in agreement with myself. *This is the time when I absolutely must write. Yes, this is very, very true.* I continue nodding and not writing.

After nodding and not writing for some time longer, it occurs to me that perhaps I need to go somewhere else to write more and nod less. Somewhere without the mesmerising view. I snap Henri shut and wave goodbye to the lovebirds, who are too in love to notice, before marching back into the day. If the words aren't going to come to me, which clearly they're not, then I will go to them. I've decided they're currently residing in Anna's office where there is a spare desk for times like this. Surely they'll show up in a professional environment buzzing with well-dressed creative people.

However while driving past Centennial Park, I make the executive decision to bypass the office and turn instead into the century-old sandstone gates. The parklands are almost devoid of cars, possibly because it's a weekday. I slow down, pulling into a shady parking space under a pine tree. There's not a loving couple anywhere in sight. In fact, the place is deserted. Perhaps nature holds the key to the missing words instead. Instantly I relax.

I may be using my environment as an excuse not to write. It wouldn't be the first time. While it's important to have a space where you feel relaxed and comfortable enough to create, I'm aware it can also be used as a clever way of getting out of doing the actual work. Often, when I've found myself stuck or unable to come up with the right turn of phrase, I've blamed it on my surroundings and gone looking for somewhere else. Naturally, this quest takes up time, time that could be better spent writing. I, therefore, like to keep any changes to my environment when writing to no more than three a day. Ideally, I stay in one spot.

The best place to write is the place where I am. Wondering if you're supposed to be somewhere other than where you are is a terrific time-waster, as is searching a real estate website for that perfect house in the country which you think will inspire you but which you're never going to buy. And let's face it, scouring travel websites for that ultimate holiday destination where you'll finally finish that novel is not going to do it either. In my experience, if you're not writing 'here' you're even less likely to write 'there'.

That said, there are always going to be times when an environment isn't conducive to being creative. Sometimes you *have* to move. Yet before I travel to some exotic destination in the hope of unlocking the well of inspiration, I set myself a challenge: to start writing where I am. Inspiration is always dancing and moving around and through us, but without the discipline to sit down and create, inspiration will only be a passing dance partner. The trick to making art is to dance wherever you happen to be.

I say this while sitting at a rickety wooden table beneath a giant and enchanting fig tree dedicated to 'Jane on behalf of family and friends'. I'm here because I convinced myself the café was too distracting, with its gorgeous view and love-struck clientele. This highlights just how crafty we human beings can be, especially when we want to get out of doing something we don't feel like doing. The café wasn't the reason I wasn't able to write, I was. Now that I know this, there's no more wriggling out of it. This is the last stop for today.

In front of me is a murky brown yet peaceful lake, alive with a cacophony of sounds from the variety of wildlife. The air is cool, and I wrap my jacket more tightly around me so that I'm not tempted to use the weather as another excuse to leave. Opening my laptop, I find myself contemplating the enormous fig tree. I have a sense of being enclosed beneath its large, outstretched branches that twist in and out like jagged, intertwined arms. The branches hang low, pulled towards the earth by gravity, unlike other branches of other trees that stretch up towards the sun.

I stare at the ground, wondering what the crooked branches are saying. I realise that often, in times of need, we look skywards for some special force or power that will help us through the uncertainty and inertia. What if the branches are saying there's an alternative?

Creativity is a physical activity. Taking an idea and turning it into something tangible requires the use of our body. Our physical being is the instrument through which creativity moves. To use our body means we must first be grounded within it. I remember hearing spiritual teacher Eckhart Tolle once say, 'the fastest way to bring our attention back to the present moment is to breathe into our *feet*'. The feet connect the body to the earth. It is the earth that supports, nourishes and provides a foundation for our bodies to continue surviving, to continue creating.

I take off my shoes and slide my toes into the dirt, closing my eyes for a few moments and feeling the tiny grains of sand. In the distance, the calls of the birds and the squawking of the nearby geese echo through the park. A cool breeze brushes gently over me. With my eyes still closed, I visualise currents of energy rising from the centre of the earth, drawing the energy through my feet and up into my body. This energy is what I need to write the words I've committed to writing. I open my eyes, my fingers hanging over the keyboard, tingling. They fall upon the letters, and the words form effortlessly.

Insight of the Day

Create where you are. If you can't, find a place where you can. Ground yourself in nature. Take off your shoes. Feel the earth beneath your feet. Draw energy from the ground. Use it to make your art.

Day 13

Why we tell stories

Three kookaburras perch in a row on a low-hanging branch of a tree in my neighbour's front garden. They are laughing, their rollicking cackle shattering the crisp morning air. I stand beneath them, my hands jammed into the pockets of my black snow jacket. 'Hello, kookies.' The laughter continues. It's like some private joke. When I turn to leave, the laughter stops. With their little beaks cocked to the side, they're aware of me. We stare at each other for a bit longer before I head down the hill to the beach as the laughter starts up again.

According to my trusty dream dictionary, seeing a kookaburra symbolises a 'wake-up call to the fires of your passion'. In Aboriginal Dreamtime folklore, the spirits decided they needed some kind of noise at dawn to 'herald the coming of the sun and waken the sleepers'. I'm one of those sleepers. The kookaburra, known as the *Goo-goor-gaga*, or the laughing jackass, was chosen for obvious reasons. The kookaburra's laugh serves as an inspiring reminder to keep the flames of our passion burning bright. I'm grateful for the early morning encouragement from my feathered friends.

While watching the changing colours of another brilliant sunrise, the birds' laughter echoing in the distance, I marvel at the mystery of life. Since beginning this creative pilgrimage, time has slowed to a crawl. My days expand outwards like a cat stretching after a nap. This new sense of spaciousness has made me more aware of the subtleties within each moment. Animals are no longer just animals. They are also messengers with secrets to share. To hear them we only need to stop and listen.

Walking along the cliff path I turn my face from the wind. Below, the ocean lies perfectly still. The world is quiet. Not even the sound of a wave tickling the edges of the rocks below disturbs the peace. I'm alone although I feel anything but. Out of the corner of my eye I notice a ripple in the water and I stop, leaning against the metal railing, waiting. A fin breaks through the surface, followed by another and then another. Tears unexpectedly spring to my eyes. As a pod of dolphins move gracefully through the water less than a hundred metres away, I remember the words of a poem I wrote as a little girl:

I love watching dolphins
Swimming through the sea
If ever I see a dolphin
I imagine it is me.

The poem was the first entry in what would become my first ever book, a collection of poems my parents collated and printed for my tenth birthday. I titled it *Poems of a Ten Year Old* and I remember holding the thin book with its pastel blue cover and feeling giddy. I had found my calling.

Watching these beautiful creatures move rhythmically through the ocean, I sense what I must have been feeling when I wrote that poem. They look so calm and peaceful, at home in their ocean playground. I long to reach out and touch their slippery, silky skin. Instead, I settle for jogging along the walkway to keep up with them as they continue their journey north.

Dolphin: *A dolphin symbolises spiritual guidance, intellect, mental attributes and emotional trust. The dream is usually an inspirational one, encouraging you to utilise your mind and move upward in life. It also suggests that a line of communication has been established between your conscious and subconscious. Dolphins represent your willingness and ability to explore and navigate through your emotions.*

When the dolphins disappear from view, I have an urge to contact the lovely shop assistant from Fine & Sonny and thank her. If it wasn't for our conversation in the store the other day, I might not have persevered with the early starts, and I wouldn't have been privy to the many morning secrets. I wouldn't have laughed with the kookaburras or played with the dolphins. I wouldn't have received their silent messages.

Coincidentally, or perhaps not, Fine & Sonny are having their official store opening this morning and Anna and I are invited. The timing is once again perfect and, after returning from the walk, I get changed and head up to Bondi Junction. I turn on the radio in the car and hear the usual breakfast banter. I'm about to change the channel when Rach, half of *The Rach and Pete Show*, says, 'Most people think they're great storytellers.' I'm intrigued.

'I'm a great storyteller,' says Pete, the show's haughty, sharp-tongued other half. 'Everyone loves my stories.'

'You have tickets on yourself,' says Rach.

'Hey, that's not me saying that. That's what people have told me.'

'Actually, that's true. You are a good storyteller,' says Rach. 'Your stories are often very funny and unexpected.'

'See? I told you.'

'Anyway, you have less than twenty seconds to capture someone's attention when telling them a story.'

'Rubbish,' says Pete. 'Where did you hear this?'

Rach laughs. 'This is what the experts say.'

'Who are these "experts"? Where did you find these people? I reckon you just made that up.'

Rach laughs again. 'Okay, well, how long would you say you have to capture someone's attention?'

'If someone's telling me a story, I'll give them five seconds, max. If they haven't got my attention by then, they're gone. I have a very short concentration span and I reckon most people are like me.'

'Okay, well, we're going to put this to the test. If you think you're a good storyteller we want to hear from you. Give us a call on 134 555 and tell us your story.'

A song plays and I leave the radio on, curious to hear the rest of the segment. I recall the conversation with Christian on the first day of this pilgrimage about being a storyteller first and a writer second. Stories are powerful mechanisms for transformation. Writing enables me to tell the stories that have changed my life and share them with others.

'Okay, so this morning we're talking about storytelling and how to be a good storyteller,' says Rach once the song has finished. 'Experts say that you have twenty seconds to capture your audience's attention while Pete is only willing to give someone five seconds.'

'And I reckon that's being generous,' Pete chimes in.

'Apparently there are a lot of people who think they're great storytellers because our phone lines are jammed. We've picked out a few callers who are going to share their story live on air and then we're going to judge their storytelling abilities.'

'We're judging?' asks Pete.

'That's right.'

'Oh God. Those poor buggers. You don't want me judging. I have no patience. I can barely stand listening to myself.'

'Okay, so who do we have first?' asks Rach.

'Hello?' says a timid voice.

'Nup,' says Pete.

Rach laughs. 'They haven't started yet.'

'I can tell by the voice they're going to be awful.'

'Don't be mean,' says Rach, hanging up on the caller and choosing another one. 'What's your name and where are you calling from?'

'My name is Sally and I'm from Penrith.'

'Okay, Sally, what's your story?' asks Rach.

'Um, well, the other day I was in the supermarket ...'

'Bzzzzz,' interjects Pete. 'Borrrrrring.'

Rach laughs. 'Sorry, Sally. I have to agree. You didn't grab me with that opening.'

'Okay, thanks. Bye.'

Rach continues, 'Next we have Nathan from Bulli. What's your story, Nathan?'

'G'day guys,' says an upbeat voice with a blokey Australian accent. 'I've got an awesome story for youse ...'

'Bzzzzz,' says Pete. 'You can't start a story by telling us how awesome it is. See ya later.'

'You're mean,' says Rach. 'You didn't even give him a chance.'

'I'm just calling it like it is.'

'Okay, well, we have a few more. Let's go to the next one. Hello?'

I park the car but keep listening. One after the other, the callers attempt to impress the hosts with their storytelling abilities only to be instantly cut off, usually by Pete who truly has no patience. No one manages to finish their story before Pete ruthlessly shuts them down. The stories are either too long, too boring or too confusing. Or all of the above. Why can't anyone keep their audience's attention?

Each caller is trying to impress, hoping to win Rach and Pete's approval. This is the quickest way of gaining their *disapproval*. When you do anything to win the approval of another, it seems to have the opposite effect. Of course, the segment was set up this way, so the callers were doomed from the start, yet it highlights how storytelling is not about trying to impress the other person. Rather, telling an engaging story means giving something of value to the listener. A story has to be offered in service of your audience, not yourself, otherwise it won't work. You'll be hung up on.

I walk to Fine & Sonny. The store is filled with a young, attractive, fashion-conscious crowd standing around sipping on flutes of sparkling wine, even though it's only nine-thirty in the morning. A knot of discomfort tightens in my stomach. I loathe turning up to social gatherings alone when I don't know anyone. It's like wading through a pool of awkward. I can't see my friendly shop assistant anywhere and I'm about to turn and make a run for it when an attractive brunette dressed head-to-toe in black appears.

'Are you here for the opening?' she asks, her plump, red lips stretching open.

I nod, introducing myself. She says she's Andrea, the PR director. 'Would you like a glass of wine?' I respond with a vigorous nod. 'So how are you connected with Fine & Sonny?'

'Well,' I say, after taking a big gulp, 'I was in here the other day with my friend and I got talking to one of your shop assistants. I wanted to come and thank her because she helped me with something but I don't know her name and I can't see her here.'

'What a lovely thing for you to do. Yes, we've a great team here.

How did she help you?'

I tell Andrea how she helped me find the motivation to get up earlier. 'Today is the second day I've woken up at five and this morning was one of the most magical experiences. Not only did I witness a spectacular sunrise, but I also got to hang out with some kookaburras and a pod of dolphins. If it weren't for your excellent employee, I would have missed it. She was like my angel.'

'That's beautiful,' says Andrea. 'You have to share that story with Courtney. She's our managing director. Come over and I'll introduce you.'

'Oh, sure,' I say, downing the last of my drink. A waiter emerges, offering a refill and I hold out my glass gratefully.

Andrea guides me through the crowd towards a tall, young, elegant woman with translucent skin. She exudes an air of confidence and authority and having caught Andrea's eye, wraps up the conversation she's having and turns around to greet us. 'Hedley has an incredible story I want you to hear,' Andrea says as a wave of self-consciousness floods my body. I remind myself of what I learnt from the radio segment earlier: don't try to impress. Make the story about your audience, not you.

Once again, I recount the story of my experience in the store a few days ago. When I finish, I notice there's a tear in Courtney's eye. 'Thank you for sharing that,' she says, placing her hand over her heart. 'Would you mind if I tell the rest of the staff? I want everyone in the company to hear it. It's a reminder of the impact we can have on others and that's what this company is about.'

'What? Now?' I take another gulp of wine.

Courtney laughs. 'No, I wouldn't do that to you. At the next team meeting. It captures precisely what we are about as an organisation and what we are trying to achieve. I think the team would really benefit from hearing about your experience. Would that be okay?'

I laugh with relief. 'Absolutely. I'd love you to.'

Over the next hour, I chat with some of the other staff and guests and even run into someone I haven't seen in years. I'm glad I stayed. I'm also quite buzzed from the alcohol I've drunk on an empty stomach. I didn't have breakfast and figuring it might be time to find some food, I say a quick goodbye to Andrea and Courtney before heading off. While walking back, I consider the power inherent in our stories, and how sharing them can help create new connections. Had I not shared my story with the shop assistant, it's unlikely anyone else would have heard it. By her not being there, I was able to share my experience with others. As a result, the enthusiasm and kindness the shop assistant bestowed on me will now be given to even more people.

Insight of the Day

Become a storyteller. Turn your stories into gifts and share them with others. Give your stories easily and freely and make them about the other person. Take the time to listen to other people's stories. Be open to receiving the gifts hidden within them.

(And always eat before drinking champagne in the morning.)

Day 14

The fear of endings

Sliding into my favourite booth at Earl's, I want to celebrate having made it to the halfway point. Over the past two weeks I've battled doubt, insecurity, laziness and boredom yet managed to churn out two thousand words, sometimes more, each day. It hasn't been easy. I can't remember the last time I did anything consistently for two weeks in a row, other than eating and showering. And sleeping, of course. Oh, and drinking coffee. So there are a few things I've done consistently but writing isn't one of them. As a reward, I order pancakes.

What am I going to do when this is over?

Fear ripples through my body.

I haven't thought about this until now, possibly because I didn't expect to make it this far. I've been too busy worrying about whether I have the commitment and ambition to finish this thing than to fret about what happens when it's over. Although now that I've reached the halfway point, it might be a good idea to start thinking about it.

So, what am *I going to do when this is over?*

Rhett arrives with a pile of white papers, which he throws on the table next to me.

'What's that?' I ask.

'It's a script for a short film I'm acting in,' he says. He slides into the booth.

'Can I have a look?' I'm already leaning over and picking up the pile of papers. 'Who are you playing?'

'Rhett.'

I scan my eyes over the lines assigned to Rhett, which include:

'You're a moron.'

'I want more time with the kids.'

'Are you serious?'

'Piss off!'

'No, you piss off!'

I hand the papers back.

'My character is this really angry ex-husband who is fighting his ex-wife over custody of the kids,' he says. 'The director is great. He keeps saying just go for it.'

'That's awesome. You're going to have fun with that one.'

Rhett pats the pile of paper. 'Sure am.'

'Hey, what about the script you're writing?' I ask. 'How's that going?'

He grabs his denim jacket and pulls it over his head, sliding down the back of the booth. I laugh. 'That bad, huh?'

'It's not as bad as I'm making out,' he says, straightening up again. 'I've almost finished.'

'That's great. So what's with the whole disappearing act you've got going on?' He buries his face in his hands. 'Hang on, I don't understand. Why are you burying your face in your hands?'

'I don't want to talk about it.'

'Is it Sophie? Did you guys break up? You looked so loved up the other day.'

'No,' says Rhett quickly. 'She's great. We're great. I don't know. I'm so close to finishing the script ...' He shakes his head. 'I don't know.'

'What do you mean you don't know. How does it end?'

Rhett remains silent.

'Do you know how it ends?' I ask, confused.

He pulls his jacket over his head again. 'I don't know. Can we talk about something else?'

'Are you *afraid* to write the ending?'

Rhett pops his head back out. 'No! I don't know. Maybe. Why are you doing this to me?'

'That's it, isn't it? You're afraid to write the ending. You know I've heard of this happening to writers. They spend so much time working on something, they become so attached to the project that just as they are coming to the end of it, suddenly they get writer's block. Or they keep tinkering with it, writing draft after draft after draft. Either way, they *never* finish.'

'It's true,' he says, nodding. 'I hate endings. They suck. I finished reading a book the other day and I was devastated. Not because of the story, but because it ended. The last few pages are hell for me. Except for relationships,' he adds quickly. 'I don't mind when those end. Not with Sophie, of course.'

'Ugh. Those endings are the worst. That dreadful feeling when you wake up and realise you have to start everything all over again. I hate that feeling.'

'Yeah, now that you say it, they are pretty shit. I've had some doozies.'

'That reminds me of something that happened not long after I first met you.'

'What's that?' says Rhett.

'We were in the middle of a conversation and I had to go. I said "goodbye" and you went to say goodbye but it was like you got bored halfway through. You were like "Goodb ... ah, forget it.' I walked out of the café thinking, "That was a really weird goodbye". Now I know why – you hate goodbyes!'

'Really?' Rhett laughs. 'I don't remember that. But you're right – I do hate goodbyes. If I had magical powers, one thing I would do is delete all pleasantries. Make "hello" and "goodbye" obsolete. How great would that be? You could just wander in and out of situations never worrying about when or if you're going to see this person again. There would be no beginnings and definitely no endings.'

'A life without pleasantries, huh?'

'Doesn't that sound amazing?'

'It sounds like you need to go write the ending to that script of yours.'

'No! I don't want to. I can't.'

'You *have* to,' I say, smiling. 'You have to face your fears. You have to write that ending. Just because you write an ending to your script doesn't mean it has to be the end. You just go and write something else. You keep writing.'

Rhett looks down. 'That's a good point. I'm going to give it a try. I'm going to go and finish that thing. Or at least get started on finishing it!'

'Yeah! You go write that ending!' I raise my palm in the air and Rhett slaps it.

'What about *you*?' he asks. 'What are you going to do?'

'I'm right in the middle so I just have to keep going. Although this conversation has helped me figure something out.'

'What's that?'

Rhett isn't the only one afraid of endings. I was just worrying about what I was going to do when this challenge is over while gorging on pancakes. I'm afraid of endings too. My greatest fear is falling back into the way things were before, when I wasn't writing. After chatting to Rhett, it doesn't have to be this way. The month of August might be over, along with my creative pilgrimage, but that doesn't mean it's the end. This particular story might be over but the writing never is. So, the question isn't, 'What am I going to do when this is over?' but rather, 'What's the next story I want to write?'

'And the answer to that is what?' asks Rhett after I share my realisation with him.

'I don't know yet. But I've got a couple of weeks to figure it out.'

'I like that. The story ends but the writing never does. You know, I think I'm ready to go and write the ending to my script now. Thank you.'

'Hey, thank *you*.'

I collect my wallet and keys as Rhett stands up and turns to face me. He looks directly into my eyes and says, 'Goodbye.'

I laugh. 'Wow. You really nailed that.'

'Thanks,' he says, beaming. 'I feel like I've come so far already.' We leave the café together and Rhett turns to wave goodbye again as he steps onto the road into the path of an oncoming bus.

'Rhett!' I yell.

He jumps back onto the curb just in time to avoid the bus which hurtles passed. 'Far out. That was close,' he says, his face a few shades paler.

'A little too close. Maybe go slowly on this ending stuff, huh?'

He laughs before setting out across the road, this time looking both ways first.

Walking slowly back up the hill towards home, I feel as if a weight has been lifted off my shoulders. One of the reasons I began this project was because I wasn't finishing anything. I was great at starting new projects but not so good at following through on them. It never occurred to me that this might not have anything to do with my capacity to commit and more to do with a fear of endings. Most of the time, endings are hard and uncomfortable. Sometimes they're painful. This is true not only of relationships but creative projects as well. As long as you're always working on something you never have to experience those difficult and unpleasant emotions. You can remain safe in your cocoon, even if it is ultimately unfulfilling.

As long as I was diving towards a notebook, or scribbling down potential characters and plot sequences and snippets of scenes, I was engaged. I was doing my art. Or at least pretending to. I could revel in the high of that bright and brilliant new idea forever even though my actual creative output was minimal. I'm constantly amazed by the stories we tell ourselves to remain protected and this could very well be one of those stories.

I've never had a problem beginning something. There's a certain thrill to beginnings, whether it's a new story, a new job or a new relationship. The experience is fresh and exciting and full of *hope*. It's as if suddenly the world is at your feet and the possibilities are endless. Anything is possible. At least it is when you're starting out. Of course, this does mean you have to remain perpetually in a state of beginning something, at the expense of ever finishing.

So what about endings?

Stephen Covey once said, 'Start with the end in mind.' Since then, every life coach and goal-setting expert has repeated this message. Well, sure. No problem. I can start anything with the end in mind because I'm *starting* and the end is only in my mind. I'll start hundreds of projects 'with the end in mind' as long as I maintain the thrill of that beginning. But the truth is no one starts something for it to end, even though it inevitably will. We don't like endings because endings mean change. Whether we know it or not, we start something for the *experience* more than the destination.

It has simply never occurred to me that I'm *afraid* of endings, and this could be the reason I often don't finish creative projects.

J.K. Rowling once said how she feared finishing her Harry Potter books because she was going to miss the characters, in particular, Harry, when it was all over. She had spent eight years with these characters, engaged in their world on such an intimate level. Suddenly, she felt apprehensive. Imagine what would have happened if J.K. Rowling had allowed that apprehension to overwhelm her?

We need endings as much as we need beginnings. When we hold onto endings out of fear of what we might lose, we hold our stories hostage. We don't set them free and we limit our creative expression. My fear of finishing this pilgrimage is muted by the act of writing every day. The end of a story doesn't mean the end of creativity; therefore, it's okay to keep going while moving closer to the finishing line and the unknown that follows it.

I check the time. It's a couple of minutes before midnight. It's the end of another day which isn't really an ending but merely a continuous changing of form. Having finished the two thousand words, my eyelids long to fall shut when they blink wide open again. *Hang on! Today isn't halfway. Tomorrow is. I'm a day and a half early.*

What the ...

How could I have got this wrong? Okay, so I was never good at maths, but dividing thirty-one in half isn't exactly a complicated equation. I'm a day and a half behind where I thought I was which means I have an extra day and a half of writing. Why am I disappointed by this? After all, I'm a writer and writing is what I love doing. So what if I'm behind? That's more time to do what I enjoy doing most. Plus, the purpose of this creative challenge was to get back into the habit of writing on a daily basis. Therefore, this is good news. It's *great* news. There is no end to this. Once I'm done with this story, another will begin. And then another. My job is just to keep writing.

Insight of the Day

Beginnings and endings are a natural part of life. They are both important. Give them equal love and attention. Ultimately, there are no true beginnings and endings anyway, just a continuous changing of form.

Part III - Determination

From Latin *determinationem* (nominative *determinatio*) 'conclusion, boundary'.

See determine.

determine (v.)

From Latin *determinare* 'to enclose, bound, set limits to', from *de-* 'off' (see *de-*) + *terminare* 'to mark the end or boundary', from terminus 'end, limit' (see terminus). Sense of 'coming to a firm decision'.

To do something.

Day 15

Staying connected

The room is empty and lit only by a light hanging from the ceiling above the large table. I wonder if I have the wrong place or the wrong day and part of me hopes I do. I'd prefer to be outside enjoying the sunshine. I poke my head through the doorway and spy an older man standing at the end of the table slipping off his jacket and hanging it on the back of a chair. 'Is this where the writers' group is meeting?' I ask. He looks up. He seems irritated by my question.

'Yes,' he says without a smile.

'Excellent,' I say, fighting the urge to turn and walk out.

'And I think it's important we acknowledge the seventieth anniversary of the end of World War II.'

I'm sorry, what?

I watch as he extracts a laptop from his black shoulder bag and places it on the table. I have no idea what he just said or for whom the statement was intended, but as I'm the only other person here, I suspect it was meant for me. But since I can't be sure, I decide to ignore it.

Minutes later another man strolls into the room in jeans and a faded T-shirt. He's younger, mid-twenties perhaps, and seems happier than Mr World War II. 'G'day, I'm Kurt,' he says cheerily, slapping his bag on the table between WWII and me. I introduce myself while WWII ignores him. He says nothing more about the war.

With Kurt here, I feel slightly more at ease and decide to stay although I choose a chair at the opposite end of the table to WWII. The three of us are silent until another man arrives. He's well-dressed in jeans and a sports jacket and introduces himself as Jasper, the co-founder of the group. Except for the look of self-importance, he has an attractive face with dark, exotic features. I guess he's in his mid-thirties.

'Right, let's get started,' Jasper says. 'The others will show up eventually. We have a few new faces so I'll give a quick rundown on how the group works and then we can get into hearing some of the ideas you've brought with you today.'

The room quickly fills as Jasper asks everyone to introduce themselves, reminding us to keep the intros brief. I appreciate his no-nonsense approach, although when it's Jasper's turn to present himself, he launches into a detailed commentary on his many qualifications, awards and achievements of which he says there are 'too many to mention'. He mentions them anyway, and I suspect he asked us all to keep our speeches brief so he didn't have to. Jasper, it appears, is very impressed with Jasper. I, on the other hand, am not.

He then invites those working on a story idea to read out their outlines. The group is then encouraged to offer feedback. As I listen to each of the ideas and the following comments, there's something about the meeting which doesn't feel right. It feels more like a murder investigation, the dim lighting adding to the solemn mood. Everyone's taking themselves so *seriously*. It's as if there's a dead body lying on the table and, one by one, each person is offering their crucial suggestion on how to bring it back to life.

'Well, we should probably focus on doing something with the heart. It looks like it could use some help,' one might say.

'Perhaps we could use our hands and start pumping?' another might call out.

'We could stab it with a needle full of steroids and shock it back to life,' suggests another.

'Who's to say they even need a heart? Why not just see what happens if you leave the heart out of it?'

'Maybe it's not a human at all but a robot disguised as a human, in which case it doesn't need a heart.'

'What if the body is alive and is travelling to another dimension and has taken its heart with it?'

I glance around the room at those sharing their feedback. No one is smiling and no one has laughed yet. I want to say, 'Hey, people! Why all the long faces? Have you forgotten why we're here? We're *storytellers*. We tell stories. Storytelling is supposed to be *fun*!' And this is what doesn't feel right about this writers' group. I'm not having any fun. No one is. The seriousness is stifling.

'Okay, I think it's time to move on,' says Jasper, with an extra dollop of seriousness. He sounds annoyed, perhaps because he hasn't done much talking about himself lately. 'Richard, you had an idea that you wanted to share?'

We all turn to look at WWII, the most serious of them all. He takes a long, solemn breath as if preparing to go into battle. 'I have an idea for a television show. It's a drama about a monkey and a cop working together to solve crimes.'

There's a moment of silence as everyone processes WWII's idea before a young man suddenly bursts out laughing. 'Cool, dude. That's funny.'

WWII turns and glares at him. 'It's not a comedy,' he snaps. 'It's a *drama*.'

The smile on the young man's face vanishes as the corners of my mouth begin to twitch.

'Does the monkey talk?' asks Gary, a writer who earlier shared a story idea about humans and aliens living together on a planet called Molotron.

WWII turns to Gary with an expression that suggests Gary's question might possibly be the most stupid and ridiculous thing he's ever heard. WWII is oblivious to the fact he's pitching an idea about a crime-solving monkey that isn't supposed to be funny. Personally, I'm with Gary. It's a legitimate question.

'No. The monkey doesn't *talk*,' WWII says, turning back to his notes while shaking his head. He seems unable to comprehend how he's surrounded by such imbeciles who evidently know nothing about television drama or crime-solving monkeys.

He's about to resume when Gary puts his hand up again. I silently applaud his bravery since WWII is clearly about to lose it. 'The reason I'm asking whether the monkey talks,' says Gary, 'is because I'm trying to figure out whose point of view the story is being told from. Is it the monkey's or his partner's?'

WWII lets out an audible sigh and I press my lips together to suppress the smile that is teetering at the edge of my mouth. I'm wondering, perhaps even hoping, if this will be the moment when WWII finally loses it. After a long pause, however, he manages to compose himself. 'How about you let me *finish* and then I will allow time for questions and answers?'

Gary nods while I take some long, calming breaths. The urge to laugh is growing more intense by the second and I'm at risk of losing it myself. WWII resumes his lecture.

'I'm sorry,' interrupts Bernie, a young hipster of about twenty who looks and sounds like he smoked a few cones before the session. 'I can't help but see this story as a comedy,' he says slowly. 'I mean, you're talking about a monkey and a guy solving crimes together. To me, that's funny, bro.'

'It's a *drama*!' barks WWII.

Bernie doesn't seem phased by the outburst while my eyes are quickly welling up with tears. I cover my mouth and bow my head.

'I just can't think of an animal show that *wasn't* a comedy,' continues Bernie.

'*War Horse!*' snaps WWII. 'That was about a horse and that was *not* a comedy. Now would you just let me finish!'

I break into a pretend coughing fit, unable to hold it together any longer. This is the most entertaining experience I've had in a long time, possibly because it's not supposed to be entertaining. I can't believe how seriously everyone is taking things.

'Unfortunately, that's all we've got time for, Richard,' says Jasper. 'We only have a few minutes before we have to wrap up and I have an idea I'd like to share.'

Oh, please no!

I check the time on my phone while drying my eyes. There are only five minutes of the session left and I doubt whether Jasper has spoken about anything in under five minutes in his entire life. Half an hour later, he's barely halfway through the story arc of his Nazi Germany blockbuster, at which point I quietly pack my bags and tiptoe out of the room.

Grateful to be out in the sunshine, I walk down to the beach, picking a spot on the grass under a large palm. I push my headphones into my ears and close my eyes as I allow the soothing voice to fill my ears. 'Nothing else but what's in front of you exists. Only what's in front of you exists. Only face what's in front of you.'

I'm listening to Matt Kahn, a spiritual teacher whose YouTube videos I find both calming and insightful. Immediately I feel the tension in my body easing. I rewind the audio and listen to the statement again.

'Nothing else but what's in front of you exists. Only what's in front of you exists. Only face what's in front of you.'

I open my eyes, curious to know what's in front of me. I see a woman wearing an orange sweater and pink fluorescent shoes bending down and taking a picture of something on a professional-looking camera. Beyond her a man gently throws a football to a toddler who's having trouble catching it. Nearby is another man carrying a little girl on his shoulders and walking in the direction of the playground. Strolling along the path next to the beach, four mothers push their prams in perfect formation. Beyond the path, the beach is dotted with sunbathers and beyond that lies the ocean, shimmering beneath the morning sun. I relax even more. All that is in front of me is very simple.

Matt's voice continues, 'If life wants you to consider something, it will arise in your experience. If it doesn't, it must not be a project you're involved in. Let the world introduce itself to you rather than going looking for it.'

The words brush gently over me like a soft, summer breeze. I love the idea of allowing the world to introduce itself. It's more relaxing than having to chase after it. Those other writers seemed to want something other than what life was introducing to them, resulting in plenty of dissatisfaction. This might have had something to do with the lack of humour in the room. Life becomes harder when you're the one who has to take care of everything, charging after it while shoving demands in its face. We don't have to do it all ourselves. Every now and then we can close our eyes and wait to see what life introduces. Ideas and inspiration have a way of showing up when we do.

Insight of the Day

We make art. We tell stories. We make music. What a gift. Feel the smile stretch across your face as you remember this and allow it to settle into your bones. Let yourself laugh. What could be more enjoyable that making something out of nothing?

Day 16

Don't forget to smile

'So how did your writing course go yesterday?' asks Mum as we head north along Military Road. We're on our way visit my cousin Norris, his wife Lou, and their two little boys, Jack and Freddie, whom I haven't seen in over three years. In reconnecting with my creativity, I've felt the urge to reconnect with loved ones, too.

'It wasn't really a course,' I say. 'It was more of a session for writers to meet and share their story ideas. It was okay.'

'Just okay?'

'Actually, it was awful. I walked out of there feeling ... sad.'

'That's doesn't sound good. What happened?'

I fill Mum in on the details. 'The group didn't really laugh,' I explain. 'But that's not what made me sad. The whole purpose was to share ideas and get feedback. But instead of listening to the comments, people kept defending their ideas. It wasn't feedback they were after; they wanted applause. When they didn't get it, they got angry.'

'That doesn't sound very inspiring.'

'It wasn't, but it gave me some valuable insights.'

The meeting made me realise I too have been taking myself too seriously, approaching writing as something I *have* to do. Writing is the one thing I love doing more than anything else in the world. It's a joy and a blessing. I'm *lucky* to be so passionate about something. Yesterday I saw what can happen when we forget why we pursue something we love doing and start expecting it to give us everything we believe is lacking in our lives. We risk ending up angry and bitter.

'I'm probably painting a slightly more dramatic picture,' I say. 'The thing is, writing, or whatever it might be, doesn't owe anybody anything. Writing doesn't owe me a living; rather it helps me navigate my experience of living. Creativity is the gift. The process of making something is what counts, not the rewards we may or may not get. Anything that comes after having made something – the money, the fame, the whatever – is a bonus.'

'That's an interesting way of looking at it,' says Mum.

'I'm just figuring this out now. Of course it'd be wonderful to earn a living from writing, but that's not why I write. I write because I love it and it gives me a sense of peace and freedom. Plus, it's fun, even when it's hard and monotonous. Ultimately, we're just telling stories. It felt like a lot of people in that room had forgotten this and it took the fun right out of it.'

For the past few years, I've been writing while living off the savings in my bank account. I've been hoping, praying, *needing* for my books to sell and my hard work to pay off. No wonder I've been so serious about writing! I've been approaching creativity as the source of my income rather than as a way to express the incoming of Source.

This is what I got from the writers' group and for this reason I'm glad I went. I'm responsible for taking care of my creativity, not the other way around. If writing isn't yet paying for my time and effort, I need to figure out a way to support myself and my creativity until it does, if it does at all. The actual writing, however, is non-negotiable. I need to write, but just because we need something doesn't mean we have to get all crazy-serious about it. Determination doesn't mean losing the lightness.

I take these insights to Anna's. She's preparing for a presentation she has to deliver next week to a group of fledgling interior designers and has asked if I could give her some feedback. I sit on a stool at the bench in the centre of her stylish kitchen.

'How do you feel about it?' I ask, cracking open a pistachio and popping it in my mouth.

'I'm freaking out,' she says, pacing up and down. 'I've got four days and I still don't know what I'm talking about.'

'Yes, you do. You're talking about your experiences as a young interior designer starting out,' I remind her. 'Public speaking is just another form of storytelling. You're just telling a story. That's all.'

She claps her hands. 'Okay. That's good. I can do that.' She stops pacing and launches into the story of how she came to be an interior designer, a story that begins in Sweden as a young protégé and continues in Australia with her own firm. I watch as she labours over a point.

'Oh God,' she says, throwing her hands in the air. 'I get so caught up in the story I forget why I'm telling it in the first place. It feels like I'm just talking about myself.'

'You are but you're doing it for your audience. Remember, no one has had your experiences, so no one knows what you know. We want to hear what it's like to walk in your shoes so that it makes walking in our own shoes a little easier. Your audience wants to listen to what you have to say. They want to know what you know but they can't if you don't share it with them. Just tell your stories and let your audience do with them what they will.'

Anna runs through her presentation a few more times until she feels confident that she's 'got it'. A few hours later, I head home even more aware how each experience is deepening my understanding of the creative process. The conversations I've had today, first with my mother and later with Anna, are conversations I would have any day of the week, conversations that would most likely be soon forgotten. This creative pilgrimage is inviting me to pay closer attention to life and in doing so, the more life is revealing about this never-ending mystery.

While I'm not a surfer, I liken my burgeoning relationship with creativity to the relationship between a surfer and a wave. A surfer will paddle out into the ocean. There, she'll rest patiently on her board while gazing towards the horizon waiting for that perfect wave. She knows a wave is coming even though she might not be able to see it just yet. When the wave does eventually arrive, she might begin paddling and kicking hard, building enough momentum to catch it and ride it into shore. Or she might just wait for the next one. Or the next, because she knows there is always another wave coming.

When the surfer does eventually catch a wave, she doesn't expect anything from it. She doesn't ride it hoping and worrying about how it's going to pay the bills. She's riding it for the pure pleasure. If she were to become excellent at riding waves, there might be people willing to pay her so she can do more of it. Naturally, she would be overjoyed by this because it would mean she could do what she most loves doing without worrying about the bills. But this isn't the reason she surfs. She does it because she loves it. As for the waves, they continue rising and falling whether she's there to catch them or not.

I'm a writer and I write because writing is my source of joy.

There's no other place where I am more at peace with myself and the world. The page is my ocean and it's where I come to ride my waves, knowing, just like the continuity of the waves, there will always be another story to write once I'm done with this one.

Insight of the Day

Creativity doesn't owe anyone a living. Creativity is the gift. Our job is to protect, support and nurture our creativity as best we can so it can continue to move, expand and express itself through us. Creativity is the expression of Source and Source is our true income.

Day 17

Unblocking the block

I begin Day 17 with a realisation: there's been a dip in my daily word count. This seems to indicate something is up. Or down rather. And it's not just my word count. My enthusiasm also appears to be dropping with every passing day. I've been writing for seventeen days straight, and if things continue at this rate, it's unlikely I'm going to make it to the end.

In *Wild*, this would be the time when Cheryl Strayed stops to remove her undersized boots and inspects the painful blisters on her feet. As one of her boots slips off the edge of the cliff and disappears into the abyss, leaving her bootless in the middle of nowhere, Cheryl questions how she's going to continue. While I might be tucked up in the comfort of my own apartment, I'm at a similar juncture, unsure of how I'm going to continue and convinced I don't want to.

Some might call this 'writer's block'. I prefer to call it a pain in the backside from which I must escape. In the past, I'd go off in search of a nail file, attack my face with a pimple popper or give my apartment a clean. I'd do any or all of these things right now as a way of getting out of writing those two thousand words. There's just one small problem: I've made a commitment.

Yet I suspect my resistance, along with my growing lack of enthusiasm, has little to do with the writing itself and more to do with the subject matter. As I think about the possibility of publishing these words, I start censoring them and myself, writing only that which I believe to be acceptable for public consumption and shoving the rest into an internal back closet.

Yet there's one story that doesn't seem to want to be locked away and forgotten about. Instead, the idea continues to taunt me like a pile of clothes on the floor that are long overdue to be washed. It's a story based on a recent cringeworthy experience which I'd rather not think about, let alone write about. Writing the story down would make it public. And that's something I'm not willing to let happen because it's embarrassing. I'm *ashamed.* And it seems my shame has become a kind of gatekeeper, refusing the exit or entry of any further creative inspiration.

I've therefore reached a creative impasse; a standoff between two thousand new words and the shameful story which I'd rather deny than write about. Now, I could just write about something else, but this becomes the point at which I bump up against that pain in the backside sensation from which I must escape. It seems until I get the words I'm refusing to write down on the page, no other words are going to grace me with their presence.

There has to be another way.

I need a space where I can write freely; a space where I can write about things that will never be published; a space where I can write without worrying about anyone else reading it; a space where I can write about personally humiliating and shameful stories. I need a journal.

I kept a journal as a young girl and recall revelling in the freedom of writing freely knowing that no one would ever see it. My journal was my haven, a place where I could go and express my innermost thoughts and desires without fear of retribution or humiliation. My diary became the place where I could indulge in my longing for Jara, an exotic-looking boy in my acting class. Or my lust for Luke, the boy who rode the same bus to school. It didn't matter, just as long as I was getting it down and out of my system. My journal was a place where I could be my honest, free and uninhibited self.

Over the years I filled hundreds of notebooks with my innermost thoughts and self-indulgent ramblings. Perhaps I stopped journalling because I became so overwhelmed by my own neuroses. Or maybe I just ran out of storage space for all the notebooks. Or maybe I fell into the trap of thinking that unless my thoughts were published – in a blog, an article, or a chapter in a book – they weren't valid. Whatever the reason, I stopped and, in turn, forgot the many benefits that journalling offers, including a place where I write privately to prepare myself to write publicly.

Pushing back the covers I roll off the bed and over to the dresser. In the bottom drawer are piles of empty notebooks I've collected over the years. I pull out a grey paper Moleskine and open it to the first blank page, smoothing my hand over the silky paper. This notebook is not Henri, a place where I write down ideas and thoughts that may or may not end up in a story. This journal is different, a place where I write for no one but myself. I'm already starting to feel lighter. Just knowing I have a private place to go.

Leaning back, my hand flies across the page as the words pour out of me like water. The story I was refusing to write sprawls itself across the page in black, incomprehensible scribbles, which is fine since I won't be reading these words again. These are not words going towards my daily quota. Instead, they are the words that are *creating the space* for the two thousand other words still to come.

I feel an immediate sense of freedom, like releasing a breath of air. Journalling has enabled me to write off the dirt and grime I've been holding onto and which has been blocking me from the real writing. No one is interested in reading everything a writer writes. I'm not interested in reading everything I write, especially when it comes to my neuroses. It's my job to know the difference between what is meant for the privacy of a diary's page and what is meant for public consumption. I realise there's a need for both.

I will always be the kind of writer who reveals more about myself than others. I tell stories mined from personal experience. These are also the stories I love to read, and which my bookshelf is full of. These are stories inspired by and written from the author's personal experience. They are real and raw; sometimes funny, sometimes gut-wrenching. By telling these stories, the authors place themselves in a vulnerable position, something I find courageous and inspiring. To write these stories, an author has to take a personal and professional risk. To write and share them comes at a price, which of course makes them all the more compelling and enticing.

These stories, when written honestly, have a purpose beyond personal catharsis. The author doesn't write them because they couldn't afford to see a therapist. These are the stories told after the author's session with the therapist and only after time and space have been allowed for healing to occur and insights to arise. Time is a great wisdom maker. Once an author has finished living a story, they are free to give it away. We still need to keep something just for ourselves. At least, I do. And what better place than in the pages of a beautiful leather-bound journal.

Insight of the Day

Keep a journal. Write in it every day. Don't censor yourself. Just write. Get as much as you can out of your head and onto the page. Create the space in which to then go and make your art.

Day 18

Making friends with media

'Is there anyone here who *doesn't* want to raise their public profile?'

My hand shoots up as I glance around the room to find my hand is not alone. This does come as a surprise. I assumed anyone attending a 'How to Market Yourself and Build a Media Profile' workshop would be more than willing to embrace such an idea. But then again, the reason most people probably sign up for such a workshop is that they're not so willing. It's certainly my reason. Hence the hand in the air.

Writing is one thing. Anyone can sit behind a computer all day, merrily tapping away on the keyboard. You can spend your whole life writing without anyone ever reading your words and you're still a writer. But what about an author? That's another game entirely. To be an author, you have to be willing to publish what you've written, thereby making it available to others. Although this still doesn't guarantee that anyone is going to know your books exist. For this, an author needs something else as well: *publicity*.

As an author, I've come to appreciate the need for an audience beyond 'family and friends', as important as that lovely and loyal category is. I also appreciate my long-held resistance towards self-promotion and publicity, which is why I thought this workshop would be helpful. After all, if I intend to continue writing books then it's essential people know about them.

The workshop leader, Prue Reece, is both a bestselling author and a media expert. Prue is not afraid of self-promotion. Her face has graced the covers of magazines and newspaper pages and she's a regular guest on television talk shows. If anyone knows how to sell herself and market a book, it's Prue. I find this both inspiring and irksome at the same time. She points to a hand sticking up in the air belonging to Phil, a first-time author from Queensland who's written a historical book about the Great Barrier Reef. 'So tell me why you don't want to raise your media profile?' Prue asks him.

'I guess I'm scared,' says Phil. 'I'm a fisherman by trade. I don't know the first thing about talking to the media. I reckon I'll screw it up and end up looking like an idiot.' Prue nods, tugging on her dark-red crêpe jacket. She looks every bit the well-rehearsed media expert. 'Well,' she says, addressing the group. 'This is why it's a good idea to get some media training beforehand. If you know you're likely to be nervous when talking to the press, media training can help you get over those fears. The fact is, to market your book you are going to need to develop your media profile. People need to know who you are so they can know to buy your book. Without a media profile, you are making life a lot harder for yourself.'

Phil nods as he continues scribbling notes in his notebook.

Prue turns to me. 'What about you, Hedley? Why don't you want to build a media profile?'

I take the microphone, aware of the forty or so pairs of eyes focused on me. 'It's not something I'm comfortable with,' I say. 'It just feels like these days everyone is trying to sell something and I'm not sure I want to be a part of it. Also, I don't trust the media.'

'Is there a reason you don't trust the media?'

I nod and tell them about *Finding Paris*. 'My words were twisted. During an interview on one of the breakfast shows, the hosts didn't even know I'd written a book.'

'It sounds like you didn't have a clear media strategy,' says Prue. 'Would this be correct?'

I nod. 'The publicity just kind of happened.'

'Which sounds good in theory,' says Prue, addressing the group once again. 'But the problem with not having a media strategy is that you become susceptible to the agenda of others. The media will always have their own agenda. As an author, you have to have one too. Being an author means taking responsibility for the sale of your books. You're all responsible for your own success. If you want people to read your book, then it helps to have the media on side. You have to understand how the media works. If you don't, then educate yourself. Learn how to give them what they need and they will help you to meet your needs. How long ago was this, Hedley?'

'A couple of years.'

'Okay, well you know what? Everyone's forgotten about it. They've moved on and it's time you did too.'

I hand the microphone back to the volunteer, shifting in my chair. Prue's words have left me unsettled, probably because I know she's right.

I didn't have a media strategy for *Finding Paris*. I didn't even know I was going to publish the manuscript until staring at the massive pile of papers held together with a bulldog clip. I hadn't even planned on writing it. One day I just started writing and the words took care of themselves. Within six months I had an 80,000-word draft. It was the most I had ever written.

Having written a very personal story, I was prepared to accept it was something that needed to be written but not published. An editor friend asked if she could read it. Two days later she called saying how much she loved it and believed it should be published. It was the encouragement I needed to move forward. Not wanting to have my story rejected by the major publishers, I bypassed them and self-published. I found an editor, a cover and template designer, a book printer, and a distributor.

Publicity came swiftly and easily. In the lead up to the book's release, I wrote a blog post about the story. A journalist from a major newspaper read the post and contacted me, asking if I'd be willing to be interviewed for an article. I agreed, and we met over coffee one sunny Saturday morning. A few months later I clicked on the newspaper's website site to find the article with my photo on the front page. The article got a lot of attention – not all of it good. The interview led to more opportunities, including the unfortunate breakfast show appearance, which I said yes to, naively abiding by the philosophy that 'all publicity is good publicity'. Eventually, when a producer of a live talk show called to inform me of a last-minute change to our previously agreed format, I decided enough was enough. I felt like sensationalised fodder. It was time to retreat and regroup.

Instead of growing my social media base, I deleted all my social media accounts. I even changed my name, deciding I was more suited to a life of anonymity than a talking head author. Since I had no further plans to publish any more books, I stopped writing. I couldn't see a point continuing. Around the same time, I began the long, slow descent into darkness from which I almost didn't emerge. I had been seeking anonymity but it had almost led to oblivion. This creative pilgrimage is helping me find my way back to a wiser and more confident version of the person I once was.

But Prue is right. The world has moved on and it's time I did too. If I'm going to be a professional author, I need an audience. Yet for an author to have an audience, the audience must know they exist. Instead of hiding behind my bad experiences, I can use them to my advantage. Instead of succumbing to the media's intention, I can take time to figure out my own. Instead of saying 'yes' to any and all opportunities, I can make a list of those I'd be honoured to have. And instead of flying blind into the world of promotion and publicity, I can educate myself so that when the time comes I can make better-informed decisions. The past doesn't have to equal the future. It's up to me to make sure it doesn't. Who knows, it might even be fun.

Insight of the Day

Some of the greatest artists of our time - Picasso, Matisse, Warhol - were entrepreneurs as well. They saw art as a business. To be a professional artist, you have to take a professional approach. Create a marketing strategy. Build a profile. Let others know you exist. See it as a challenge.

Day 19

Passion and struggle

Rhett's sitting at the back of Earl's, head bowed over some pieces of crumpled paper. He looks up and greets me with a smile. 'Hey, what are you up to?'

'I was going for a walk but then I got distracted by the thought of coffee. Can I join you?'

'Of course,' he says. 'So what's the theme this week?'

'Determination.'

'Sounds serious.'

'Actually, I'm realising it doesn't have to be. In fact, if you can have fun with something you're determined to achieve you're more likely to achieve it.'

'I like the sound of that.'

'Me too. Although it's not always easy to put into practice. I thought it would get easier to write two thousand words a day, but it's getting harder. I've been going to bed at midnight because I have to finish my words.'

'Good on you. That's inspiring.'

'Thanks but it doesn't feel like it.'

'So I tried to write my ending the other day.'

'That's great.'

'Not really,' says Rhett. 'I couldn't do it. I realised you were right. I really do have a fear of endings.'

'Now that you're aware of it you can move through it. All you need to do is sit down and do it.'

'I thought you'd say something like that.'

'Well, I am speaking from experience. It's much easier to start a creative project than it is to finish it. When you're finished, your work is at risk of being judged and criticised and who wants that? I totally get why you don't want to finish your script. I haven't finished half of the books I've started which is why it's so important I finish this.'

'Well, I'm determined to finish it now. I won't be able to forget about it until I do.'

'Determination is the theme of the week.'

'And so it is,' says Rhett, smiling.

'So what are these?' I ask, nodding at the pieces of paper Rhett had been studying before I interrupted.

He tells me about the TV commercial he's auditioning for later that afternoon. 'You can help me learn my lines,' he says, handing me the sheets of paper. The commercial is for a dating website and Rhett's character has to interview a number of potential partners.

'I'd love to,' I say, pretending to get into character.

We laugh our way through several attempts before I hand the pages back. 'That was fun.'

'Have you ever thought about giving acting a go?' asks Rhett.

'Actually, I did once. When I was younger. I loved it and was always doing acting courses in my school holidays.'

'Why didn't you stick with it?'

'On the first day of this one course – I must have been about fourteen – the teacher invited us each to mime a scene. I volunteered to go first and when I was done the teacher turned to the group and said, "Well that was boring, wasn't it?" I was humiliated. I left at lunchtime and never went back.'

'That's horrible,' says Rhett. 'What a shitty thing for a teacher to say.'

'Later, when I was twenty-two and living in Los Angeles, I tried out for the Lee Strasberg School of Acting. I needed a visa to stay in the country and I'd heard the easiest one to obtain was a student visa. So, I auditioned and got in.'

'Wow. That's a great school.'

'I know. I could have got a visa to stay in the States and pursue acting again but instead I said no. I still can't believe I didn't accept the offer. Sometimes I wonder what would have happened if I had.'

'You probably would have done well.'

'Maybe. Who knows?' I shrug. 'As you know, it's a tough industry even with the best training.'

'Like most creative professions.'

'Exactly. To pursue an artistic career, you have to be more than just passionate. I was passionate about acting but it wasn't enough to overcome one shitty comment by one shitty teacher. You've got to be able to withstand all the knockbacks and the criticism if you're going to have any chance of being successful. With writing I'm passionate but it's more than that. It doesn't matter what anyone says, I'll never give it up.'

Rhett nods. 'Yeah, I get that. It's the same for me with acting. It's definitely a struggle at times and there are times I wonder why on earth I keep going but somehow I do. If you're passionate about something *and* you have the determination to ride out the hard times, then you've got a shot because there are definitely going to be a lot of them.'

'Hey, I like that. Determination is when passion meets struggle.' I glance down at my phone. 'Oh no! I've got an appointment. I've got to run.'

Grabbing my wallet and keys, I say goodbye to Rhett and race back up the hill. Half an hour later, I'm stepping out of an elevator on the twenty-fourth floor of an office block in Bondi Junction. It occurred to me on the ride up that this is not an appointment I'm exactly excited about, having cancelled it three times already. IVF Australia.

I stand behind a loving couple who are leaning over the reception desk, as four attractive, uniformed women study the computer screen in front of them. They appear to be solving a problem for the young couple. I wait patiently until one of the receptionists calls me forward. 'How can I help you?' She moves to another computer.

'I have an appointment with Dr Collins.' I give her my name and place a polite smile on my face.

The receptionist scans the computer before sliding a clipboard across the counter. 'Great. Can you fill out these forms and bring them back to me when you're done. Dr Collins won't be too long.' She points to the waiting room which looks out across Sydney Harbour towards Watsons Bay.

'Do I need to fill out all of it?' I ask, assessing the mountain of paper.

'If you wouldn't mind.'

I take a seat opposite another young couple who are holding hands while bent over the same papers. My belongings fall onto the glass table with a crash and the couple looks up at the same time. Burying my head in the paperwork, I work through the list of personal questions.

1. What are your reasons for being here today? *I forgot to cancel and I didn't want to lose the deposit.*

2. What is your marital status? *Depressing.*

3. Is your partner supportive of your decision to explore fertility treatment? *Refer to previous answer.*

4. Have you been pregnant before? *It was supposed to be a game of tennis. Things got out of hand.*

5. Have you had an abortion? *Yes. Refer to previous answer.*

I return the clipboard to the receptionist before sitting down again where I continue wondering and making up stories about the two couples in the waiting room. How long have they been trying to conceive? Have they started IVF yet? Where are they in their cycle? Are they hopeful? Are they disappointed? Will their relationship last? How did they meet? Will they break up if they can't have a baby? Why are there only couples here? Why am I the only single person? Why am I here? Is there a sushi place nearby? I'm hungry.

'Hedley?'

A tall brunette wearing a sleek navy blue suit and another welcoming smile is standing on the other side of the waiting room, holding the clipboard carrying the pages of my life story. I smile, rounding up the items on the table. Several of them fall to the floor and the couple looks up again. 'Sorry about that,' I say to the woman while attempting to shake her hand without dropping anything else.

'No problem,' she says. 'I'm Dr Collins. Come this way.'

Dr Collins' presence is instantly calming and I like her immediately. She leads me down a long corridor before inviting me into an office with an equally spectacular view of the city. 'Take a seat,' she says, walking around to the other side of the desk. She's much younger than I would have imagined for someone in her role. Late-thirties perhaps, although she carries herself with the confidence of someone a lot older. 'How can I help you today?'

'Well,' I say, taking a deep breath. 'I'm thirty-seven and apparently I should be thinking about having children, although I don't have a partner and I'm not sure I want kids.'

Dr Collins opens the folder in front of her and begins taking notes. 'Go on,' she says.

'My friends have been gently suggesting that if I do want kids then I should start looking at my options. And they're probably right. I don't want to get to forty and regret not having done something earlier. So, I thought it was best to just come in and have a chat.'

'Good idea. The way I see it you have two options. Actually you have three. The first option is to not do anything and wait until you do meet someone. At that point you can decide to try to get pregnant naturally or go through IVF. Obviously, the chances of falling pregnant after thirty-five greatly diminish, plus IVF is not a guaranteed way to have a baby. That's one of the big misconceptions about IVF. It doesn't cure the age factor.'

'Okay.' *Should I be taking notes?*

'The second option is to freeze your eggs. That's expensive, invasive and again, it's not a guarantee. That might be something you're interested in. Your third option is to go it alone through our donor sperm program. Now, that's a big decision and it's not something you want to take lightly. To do that you have to really be *determined* to be a mother.' *There's that word again.* 'Although once again, it isn't a guarantee.'

After my recent conversation with Rhett around the meaning of the word, it pierces through the cloud of confusion I've been feeling around this issue. The knot of tension in my shoulders begins to dissolve. I know what I need to do. Or rather, not do. 'Thank you. That's very helpful.'

'Did you have any other questions?'

'No. But just out of curiosity, do you see people like me often?'

'All the time. It's very normal at your age. Having a baby is a big responsibility and to go through any of these options, it's something you have to really want. Have you tried online dating?' I pull a face and she laughs. 'I know what you mean. Most people meet their partner through work or friends. What do you do?'

'I'm a writer.'

Dr Collins frowns. 'Oh well, that doesn't help matters.'

'Tell me about it! The only guys I meet on a regular basis are the ones who make my coffee.'

Dr Collins shrugs. 'Hey, it's an option.'

I shake my head. 'It's not. Trust me.'

'Gotcha! What about joining a writers' group?'

'Been there too. But not in that way. No, I think I need someone a little ... less like me. Like an accountant, perhaps.'

'Well, there are plenty of those around. Where do they hang out?'

I shrug. 'Accounting conferences? And I'm hardly going to be hanging out at one of those.'

'If it's any consolation, I think you're a great catch. There's definitely someone out there especially for you. Let's just hope he shows up soon.'

'Thanks, Dr Collins. I'm glad I came to see you.'

'My pleasure. If you do change your mind, I'm always here.'

Stepping out into the afternoon sunshine, I feel a profound sense of relief knowing that I just don't possess the *determination* to pursue parenthood right now. I'm not passionate about having children the way some women are, and I never have been. I decide to let nature take its course and get back to what I *know* I'm passionate about: those next two thousand words.

Insight of the Day

Passion alone is not enough. Determination is also required to get you through the difficult and challenging times that are an inevitable part of any artistic pursuit.

Day 20

The magic of imagination

Settling into my seat, I open the copy of *Red Dog* by Louis de Bernières. I found it in my bookshelves next to an out-of-date *Lonely Planet* guide for Mexico. *Red Dog* is a small book, perfect for the hour-long flight to Melbourne. I flick through the pages before landing on the one with a small black-and-white photograph of the author. Across the aisle, a couple are settling themselves into their seats. I glance over at the man who looks a lot like the man in the black and white photograph. He's tall and balding with a full face and rosy cheeks. *But it couldn't be. Could it?*

By the time the doors have closed and the flight attendants have performed their cross-check, I'm absolutely convinced it is. The man across the aisle is Louis de Bernières, author of the book I'm currently reading. Of course, there's a slight possibility it's not Louis and one glance across the aisle is all it would take to confirm my suspicions (or not), but that's a risk I'm not willing to take. It's more fun to *imagine* it is Louis, the great author.

I lift my book slightly higher so it's in his direct line of vision. If it is Louis, then he'll see I'm reading his book and no doubt make some kind of gesture, like a tap on the elbow or an 'excuse me' and an offer to sign it. When there's no tap on the elbow, I raise the book a little higher. A voice in my head points out the ridiculousness of this but I ignore it, more excited by the idea of sitting next to a bestselling author whose book I just happen to be reading.

As the plane prepares for take-off, the book is practically positioned over my head like an umbrella. Yet there's still no tap. I run through the various responses I might use once I feel that finger on my elbow. I imagine turning around to find Louis smiling, giving a single nod towards the book with a pen in hand ready to sign. I would gasp in surprise before gratefully handing over my book. 'Who would you like me to make it out to?' he would ask and I would give him my name. Perhaps I'd mention that this isn't the first time he's signed a book for me, which he may or may not find interesting. I would graciously accept the book back and a fascinating conversation might ensue.

When the plane has reached its cruising altitude, the tap on my arm still hasn't come. This doesn't necessarily mean the man next to me is not Louis de Bernières. It simply means he's more modest than I've given him credit for. He's probably an introvert, preferring to avoid attention rather than inviting it with a random tap on a stranger's elbow, even if she is reading one of his books. I wonder what I would do if I noticed another person reading one of my books? The thought gives me chills. I'd be thrilled, overwhelmed with pride and joy. But would I make my presence known? Would I interrupt them with a tap on the elbow and a, 'Hey, look it's me! Would you like me to sign your book?' When I put it like that, no! I wouldn't be that presumptuous.

I return to my imaginary conversation with Louis if he were that presumptuous, which he's probably not. 'So you're heading down to Melbourne for the Festival, I presume?' he will ask, in a deep, intelligent voice.

'Oh my goodness ... Is it really ... are you ... Louis de Bernières?'

Although I probably won't say his full name since I'm not entirely sure how to pronounce it. So, I'll probably go with, 'Wow. Are you Louis?' while pointing to the name on the cover of my book. He will nod, his rosy cheeks brightening ever so slightly. His wife will probably roll her eyes and turn to stare out the window. No doubt she has come across her husband's gushing fans before.

'I can't believe this,' I will say. 'I am reading your book and here you are sitting next to me. What are the chances?'

Louis will smile or perhaps even chuckle before asking, 'So what do you do?'

I don't actually want him to ask this question. This is my least favourite question. Well, my *second* least favourite. My least favourite question is the one that comes after I've told people I'm a writer. 'Oh and *what* do you write?' is the inevitable question for which I still don't have a succinct answer. 'A little bit of this and a little bit of that' doesn't seem to cut it and nor should it. I make a mental note to explore that later. But for now, back to the conversation with Louis which is just getting started.

He might then ask what genre I prefer.

'Mostly non-fiction,' I'll say. 'But I want to have a go at fiction as well. Are you working on anything at the moment?'

'Oh yes,' he'll say, giving me a full rundown of his latest masterpiece.

I will appear interested and ask questions to keep him talking. He will reply in detail, his eyes sparkling as his idea comes to life. The protagonist of his story will have a name like Zed or Romulus and will have endured a difficult life that began with his mother dying during childbirth. Or something along those lines. I can't wait to hear all about it. *Why hasn't he tapped me on the elbow yet?*

His wife will have warmed up by now, having realised I'm not flirting with her husband and instead am just a passionate writer who is slightly star-struck at sitting next to the author of the book I'm currently reading. Surely she will marvel at the coincidence. How could she not?

My thoughts are interrupted by an update from the captain. It strikes me that I've spent the last ten minutes having an imaginary conversation. I flick to the back of the book where there's a short biography underneath the black and white photo, and I'm surprised to discover Louis is English. I had assumed he was Australian. After all, he wrote a book about a dog living in the Australian desert. This does throw a metaphorical spanner into my imaginary works as the man beside me has an unmistakable Australian accent. I know from my attempts to eavesdrop on their conversation. Also, on further thought, Louis de Bernières is scheduled to give the opening address for the Writers Festival in less than two hours. It's unlikely the Festival organisers would book their star attraction on a last-minute flight.

The evidence is mounting that the man next to me is not the great author. I'm just about to turn back to my book when I feel a light tap on my arm. Slowly I turn around. The man is holding out a pen and just when I think he's offering to sign my book he says, 'I think you dropped this.'

—

At the end of Louis' opening address at the Melbourne Town Hall some hours later, with no further plans for the evening, I decide to join the end of the long queue waiting to meet the author and have their books signed. As Louis took the stage, I noticed he bore a striking resemblance to the man on the plane, the only significant difference being his cream-coloured linen suit and light pink shirt. If it weren't for Louis' suit and distinct English accent, he could have easily been the guy sitting next to me.

While standing in the queue listening to the chatter, I realise this is not something I usually do. I'm not usually someone who willingly stands in queues, yet since beginning this creative pilgrimage, I've noticed an attitude shift. I'm saying yes to things I wouldn't ordinarily say yes to. As a result, it's coaxing me out of my shell and I'm engaging more with life. While I'm tired, I'm also excited and inspired. The more I keep showing up to life the more life turns up for me.

The most noticeable change, however, has been the pace at which life moves. Previously, days would fly by like the view through the window of a speeding train. I would arrive at the end of the day, wondering where it went, having not achieved half of what I set out to. Today, this is not the case. The last few weeks have been a slow and gentle amble until arriving at the day's end and I fall into bed, satisfied. I'm achieving what I set out to achieve and I feel richer and more fulfilled as a result.

Inching closer towards the front of the queue, I pull from my bag *Labels*, the little orange book that Louis signed for me back in 1998. A publicist is standing beside him, holding a clipboard and wearing a scowl. She flicks her hand, ushering me forwards. Louis glances up and offers a smile that doesn't quite reach his eyes. I place the book in front of him and watch as his gaze lands on his signature from years earlier. 'Did we meet in Adelaide?' he asks, looking up.

'No. It wasn't me,' I reply. 'You met my father. He gave the book to me.'

'I must have signed it with my right hand,' he says. I nod, unsure of how to respond to this unusual piece of information. 'This time I'll sign it with my left hand.'

Oh. Okay.

He snaps the book shut and hands it back to me. I thank him as the still-scowling publicist directs me towards the door. It's certainly not the conversation I had imagined. But after all we shared on the plane earlier, it was always going to be anticlimactic. I wonder how I would go with writing fiction; it certainly seems my imagination has a knack for making things up. It's a possibility I decide to ponder further over a glass of red wine and a small plate of Spanish meatballs in a half-empty bar on Elizabeth Street, just around the corner from my hotel.

Insight of the Day

Hang out in your imagination on a daily basis. Play. Daydream. Make up stories. Go wild. If people call you crazy, nod in agreement and pull a face. Let them know you wouldn't have it any other way.

Day 21

A good approach to writing

Day 21 begins just like any other: in search of coffee. Although the search is that much more exhilarating because this is Melbourne and Melbourne *is* coffee. It's in the city's DNA. I have high expectations, which is risky since there's a greater chance of them not being met. There's only one opportunity for the first taste of that freshly brewed holy grail. I have to get it right. I stop by the concierge desk on my way out.

'Good morning, ma'am,' says the same young man who provided me with directions to the Town Hall the previous evening. 'What can I do for you?'

'I'm heading to the Wheeler Centre and I'm wondering where I can get a really good coffee?'

'Certainly.'

'I don't mean just a really good coffee,' I add. 'I mean a *really* good coffee.'

He nods, appearing to understand the seriousness of my request.

He disappears behind the desk, re-emerging with a map and a pen. I can tell by the precision and confidence with which he moves, he *knows*. I can trust him.

'You want to go to The League of Honest Coffee,' he says, drawing little arrows on the map towards the location of my treasure, then marking it with a little cross.

Taking the map and sliding it into my bag, I thank him, before slipping into the crisp morning. Jamming my hands into my jacket pockets, I turn left and march on in the direction of caffeinated gold. I'm a woman on a mission. And it's a mission that is time and taste sensitive.

Pushing open the glass door, my eyes land on the young man standing behind the counter and in the 0.0000000067 seconds our eyes remain connected, a surge of electrical current shudders through my body. I'm not sure if it's the guy or the promise of coffee that has caused this reaction. Although it's likely there's a correlation between my love of coffee and the attraction I often feel towards the young men making it.

Inching closer towards my latest barista crush I'm about to deliver my order when another staff member intercepts. His face has been hijacked by a beehive of hair which moves up and down when he talks. 'What can I get you?' his beard mumbles.

'A latte and a ham and cheese croissant, please,' I say, feeling the heat emanating from the beautiful barista beside him.

I proceed to the large communal table in the centre of the café which is decorated with alternative magazines: *Oyster*, *Frankie*, and others. I can feel the barista's gaze burning into my back. This could also be my overactive imagination at play again. I retrieve Henri from my bag and open to a fresh page when I'm distracted by a shadow. I look up to see my man crush looking down, smiling. I smile back. For a moment we remain in perfect smiling silence.

'Are you ...?' he says, before pausing.

I wait for him to finish the sentence, which I'm hoping is anything from:

'... single?'

'... from around here?'

'... free tonight?'

'... free for the rest of your life?'

'... up for making babies? Or at least trying to?'

Yes, it's a question brimming with possibilities. He opens his mouth. '... ready to order?'

'Oh. I've already ordered.'

He nods before turning away. Once again reality hasn't quite lived up to the potential, which is further confirmation I should explore writing fiction.

My attention swings back to one of the magazines on the table. I pick it up just as my coffee arrives, so I place it back down to focus on the cup of heaven before me. I inhale the fresh smell of roasted coffee beans and bring the steaming liquid to my lips. The hotel concierge did well. It was worth the walk. After a few more sips, I pick up the same magazine again, yet this time my food arrives, and I place it back on the pile once more. My attention keeps returning to the magazine, and eventually, it falls on a name printed on the cover in big, white letters. Dr Elliot Rutherford. I feel a chill, although this time it has nothing to do with the barista. Dr Rutherford was a good friend of my father's. Suddenly I sense the presence of Dad. The thought makes me smile.

—

I'm still thinking about Dad as I slip into one of the empty seats in the Wheeler Centre for the first session, *So You've Published a Book*. The speaker is Graeme Simsion, author of *The Rosie Project*. Graeme was my father's name. I smile again to myself.

I don't know what happens to us after we die but I sense it's not the end. In the eight years since my father's death, I've felt his presence enough to know our loved ones are still with us after they die. I remember a friend once telling me 'Death is like the changing of channels. You have to learn how to communicate differently. It's like learning another language.' Except this language is one of signs and symbols and intuitive sensations.

For the next couple of hours, I listen as Graeme shares his knowledge about book promotion. He speaks quickly and directly as if giving a lecture on chemistry. He explains how the success of *The Rosie Project* was not about brilliant writing or the backing of a major publisher alone, but by taking full responsibility. 'You have to know the numbers of your readership, and if you don't know, then it's up to you to find out. No one is going to sell your book the way you can. It's up to you to know who is reading your book and where in the world they are.' It's clear that Graeme is as committed to increasing his readership and the sales of his books as he is to the actual writing of them. Success isn't just about luck, but rather a combination of skill and science. You can write a great book, but without an effective, well-planned marketing strategy, no one is going to know about it. I have to write fast to keep up.

The more I listen, the more comfortable I'm becoming with this idea of building a public profile. To be an author and make a living from it requires people knowing who you are and where they can find your books. Graeme's driven by a genuine desire to be of service to others, in particular, new writers, as much as he's committed to his publishing success. While pacing the front of the stage, hands active and eyes ablaze, he enthuses about how much he enjoys his success, which enables him to share his knowledge and experience with other authors. By increasing his profile, he's able to help more people.

He doesn't like to waste time, preferring to get straight to the point. 'Despite everything I've said, the best publicity is word of mouth. Write the best book you can write and don't let anything get in the way of that.'

It's simple, straightforward advice and I like it. That I can definitely do.

Write the best book you can possibly write and don't let anything get in the way of that.

After the session, I bounce back out into the Melbourne cold. All I have to do is write the best book I possibly can and not let anything get in the way of that. *I can totally do that!* As I head along Swanston Street towards Federation Square swinging my bag beside me I catch sight of a homeless man lying in an alcove. He's wearing a hood over his head and his right foot is shaking slightly. In front of him is a sign resting against a paper cup: *Homeless. Please help.* He's leaning over a piece of paper, colouring in a picture with an orange pencil. My heart leaps but I continue walking. A few metres on I stop and turn around. Pulling out a five-dollar note, I place the money in the paper cup. I wait for him to look up. I want to connect with him. But he remains focused on staying inside the lines of his drawing. He's busy being creative.

I've just helped out a homeless man doing his art. I'm a good person. I'm someone who supports the arts. I'm so impressed with myself and my display of goodness I almost don't notice the second homeless person. This time it's a young woman sitting cross-legged on a dirty blanket. Her hair is in dreadlocks and there's a streak of dirt down one side of her face. In front of her is a similar cup with a similar message: *Please help. Need money.* She's strumming a guitar.

Fresh from my last 'good Samaritan' act, I pull out my wallet again. There are two fifty-dollar notes tucked inside. *Shit!* I pretend to look for something else before snapping my wallet shut and taking off down the street. I'm struck by an overwhelming sense of shame. *A good person, huh?* Well, I am as long as it doesn't cost me more than a fiver. *Why couldn't I just give her the fifty?* So much for supporting the arts. I wander into the next session feeling deflated and disappointed in myself.

The final session for the day is *Ask a Novelist* and the guest is headliner, Louis de Bernières, although this time the stage is much smaller, as is the audience. I choose a seat towards the back of the room as Louis settles into his red leather chair opposite the interviewer. Louis is wearing a similar cream suit to the one he wore last night and the look of a well-seasoned author who's done this a thousand times before. He positions the microphone underneath his chin.

'I see myself as a poet first,' he says as the interview gets underway. 'Have you heard of Constantine Cavafy's poem, *Ithaka*?'

I feel a jolt inside my chest. *Ithaka* was my father's favourite poem, words he aimed to live his life by while encouraging me to do the same. He would recite the poem, if ever I was going through a difficult time. I read *Ithaka* at his funeral and, in the years since, I read it to myself whenever I want to feel close to him. It's been a long time since I've felt this close to my father in the years since his death. Louis begins reciting the first few lines of the poem as my heart continues to thump.

As you set out for Ithaka
hope the voyage is a long one,
full of adventure, full of discovery.

Louis stops and looks up at the audience. '*Ithaka* is the destination,' he says. 'Don't be in a hurry to get there. *Ithaka* is a good approach to take to writing.'

Ithaka is a good approach to take to writing.

It's exactly the sort of thing my father would have said.

Insight of the Day

'Write the best book you can possibly write and don't let anything get in the way of that.'

Part IV - Sacrifice

Comes from two Latin roots, *sacer*, meaning 'sacred', and *facere*, meaning 'to make' or 'to do'. In other words, 'to make sacred'.

Day 22

A way home

I wake from the most vivid dream. I was driving along a freeway when I noticed Sylvester Stallone, Arnold Schwarzenegger and Bruce Willis taking a nap by the side of the road. Sylvester was dressed as Rocky, with a tattoo that covered an entire bicep. Arnold was dressed as the Terminator, while Bruce was just Bruce. I can't remember what he was wearing. I thought a conversation with the three movie stars would provide inspiration for my two thousand words, so I stopped the car. Strolling up to three Hollywood heavyweights for a chat isn't something I would normally do. I realised it was because of this creative pilgrimage. I was developing courage, as well as many other qualities. Unfortunately, I woke up before getting to talk to the stars.

Wrapped up in the crisp bed sheets, a knot of tension rises in my stomach. I roll over and reach for my phone. It's 6.36 am. It's three hours before the first session of the day so I roll back over and stare up at the ornate ceiling. Suddenly my thoughts make an unexpected detour back to *that* night in February. It was less than six months ago yet I'm surprised by how little I think about it. I shouldn't be here. I almost wasn't here. And yet, here I am, lying in a hotel bed, in Melbourne for the Writers Festival, having a wonderful time, living my life as if that night never happened.

The first thing I remember was the sound of a voice whispering in my ear. It was a female voice, a gentle voice. 'Hedley,' it said quietly. 'Your mum is here.'

My eyes were heavy. Opening them was like winching up an anchor from the ocean floor. My vision was blurry and I could just make out the colour green. I was wearing something green. Tubes were everywhere, wrapping themselves around me like tentacles. Blurry figures rushed past. A woman in blue holding a clipboard stopped by my bed, looked at something and disappeared. The room was full of machines. Lots of machines. I lifted my eyes and saw my mother looking down. Her expression was serious but calm. She bent over, put her arms around me and I leaned into her, sobbing lightly. I didn't have to ask where I was.

The next time I opened my eyes, my surroundings were different. The room was much smaller and white. Everything in the room was white, including the few items of furniture – a table, a chair tucked beneath it and a cupboard. The only colour came from the green gown I was still wearing and my mother who was standing at the table folding clothes. She was wearing grey jeans and a patterned shirt. I vaguely recall eating something before my eyes closed again.

I'm told I met with three doctors while I was in hospital although I only remember one. He was a tall, grey-haired man with kind eyes. I liked him immediately even though I didn't trust him. After all, he was a psychiatrist who was going to insist on some mental health program that would inevitably include antidepressants, even though I was not depressed. Not now. Not after being given a second chance. On the inside, beneath the fog, I was filled with gratitude. This wasn't something I wanted to mute with medication. Of course, trying to convince any medical professional that I didn't require medication having just attempted suicide was always going to be an uphill battle.

The doctor filled me in. 'You were in ICU for three days. You were then transferred to the mental health ward which is where you are now. You've been in hospital for almost a week. You do realise you shouldn't even be here right now?'

I nodded.

'It's lucky you called the ambulance when you did.' I nodded again. 'So why don't you tell me what happened?'

I spoke in a wobbly voice. My ability to think clearly was still impaired and my thoughts were slow and laboured. I attempted to explain the events that unfolded that night, even though I didn't fully understand what happened. I explained the dark thoughts I'd been having six months earlier that had given rise to the request for the Valium, but also that I'd had these thoughts before and never acted on them.

'Can you recall anything that you were doing differently at this time?'

I shook my head. Nothing came to mind. I did mention the growing sense of homesickness. Not surprisingly, the doctor didn't know what I was talking about.

'Have you ever been homesick?' I asked him. He nodded.

'Well, I've been having this feeling of homesickness for a while now, but it's a thousand times more intense. Suicide wasn't my objective, although I knew that's what I was doing. It's not that I wanted to die. I wanted to go *home*. As in, *home* home.'

'What do you mean?'

'I don't know how else to describe it. I've always sensed there's more to the world than what our physical senses tell us. We come from somewhere and when we die we return to that somewhere. I don't know where or what that is but I don't believe this world is all there is. I sense there's more. When we die, we are liberated from the restrictions and limitations of being in a body. We're free at last, again. We return to perfect peace. I can sense it, taste it, it's this feeling on the tip of my tongue. It's right there, but I can't quite grasp it. So, it's not that I wanted to die, I just wanted to go *home.* I wanted to feel peace again.'

I'm not sure whether the doctor understood what I was talking about, perhaps because I wasn't sure I fully understood it myself. This was something I could feel but not necessarily put it into words. I also told him that when I hear about someone passing away, part of me feels a little envious. My sadness is for myself and those who they've left behind, not for them. They are the lucky ones. Their spirits are free once more. My sense is life is backward, like the negative of a film. We cry at funerals and celebrate at births even though the moment we are born, our suffering is guaranteed. Our happiness, on the other hand, isn't. Instead, this becomes a choice. Unfortunately, many of us don't realise this until later in life, having endured our fair share of disappointments and decided 'enough is enough' and we take back our lives, placing it in our own hands, or God's. Or we don't and remain victimised by our own suffering.

'There's one thing I'm absolutely certain of now,' I told the doctor.

'What's that?' he asked.

'Life is the point. Life is the whole experience, the good and the bad. If we had only the good, then what's the point? I've spent much of my life longing "to go home" but this is exactly what's been holding me back from being fully here. Keeping this option open has kept me from living the best life possible. By holding onto the idea that I could check out if it ever became too hard meant I've never really checked in.

'But this all changed the minute I swallowed those pills. Suddenly the choice was taken out of my hands. I knew I'd crossed a line I wasn't supposed to cross. At that moment, everything became clear. There's a reason we don't know when our lives are going to end because we're not supposed to know. If we did, we wouldn't be able to have the full experience of life. We're all going to die at some point but it's not up to us to decide when that will be. It will happen when and how it happens. In the meantime, it's up to us to make the most of what we have while we're here. I know this now and I want this now. I'm committed. As long as I'm here on this earth, I'm committed to experiencing life in all its guises. I want life in its entirety and I'm willing to accept it – the good and the ugly. Yet I couldn't have known this without taking those pills.'

'You do realise that most people who do what you did don't get to make that choice again? They don't get a second chance.'

I could feel the tears coming and I grabbed a tissue from the box on the side table.

The doctor continued, speaking softly. 'What you did was very serious, Hedley. You crossed a line. People cross that line all the time and they don't get a second chance. They don't get to have the realisation you're now having. They don't get to choose again. You're incredibly lucky. Do you understand what I'm saying?'

'That's why I'm not going to throw it away,' I said. 'Yes, I made the decision to take the pills but I also made the decision to call the ambulance. I'm here because I *want* to be here. It's the first time in my life I can genuinely say that. I *want* to be here and I know how lucky I am to be here. I'm not going to mess that up.'

The doctor eyed me for what felt like a long time.

'I promise,' I added. 'I've never felt so sure about anything in my life. I'm not the same person who took those pills. Something inside me has changed. This is the truth.'

This was the truth. I'd been given my life back and I wanted to be here. Aside from the fogginess and lingering headache, I felt clearer than ever. I knew the days and months ahead weren't going to be easy, but I was prepared to face them. For the first time I was willing to accept life on life's terms. I'd take the good, the bad and everything else because this is what life is. Yes, there would be hard times. Yes, there would be lonely times. Yet these times no longer frightened me, nor were they experiences I felt I needed to avoid or escape. I felt capable of confronting these times in the same way everyone has to. Life isn't perfect and no one has a perfect life. It's foolish to think otherwise. In fact, it's dangerous. I could no longer keep carrying around that card in my back pocket as a 'last resort'. Life was the resort.

I was discharged from hospital a week later.

—

Wrapped up in my hotel bed, I'm again surprised by how little I've thought about that night. It was less than six months ago, yet it feels like a dream. Except of course it wasn't a dream. It was real and it happened and I need to remember this so that it never happens again. I wouldn't have had the realisation that I've had if I hadn't taken those pills. But surely there's another way?

As you set out for Ithaka
hope the voyage is a long one,
full of adventure, full of discovery.

I think about the two homeless people I saw on the street yesterday: the man colouring in and the woman playing the guitar. I marvelled at their capacity to keep going in the face of what seemed like great hardship. What did they have that I had lacked on that night back in February? They had some purpose, a reason to live despite being without the basic comforts most of us take for granted. They were creating for no apparent reason or outcome.

Was this it? Was the act of colouring in or playing music the thing that was keeping them going? Did creativity have the power to bring us back from the brink? Was it enough to put broken lives back together, or at least just keep them going? Could creativity ward off the darkness? And by engaging with creativity on a regular basis, could we turn our lives around?

I remember the question the doctor asked me. 'Can you recall anything that you were doing differently at this time?'

I couldn't answer the question then but I can now. Although it wasn't what I was doing differently. Rather, it was what I *wasn't* doing.

I wasn't writing.

I've been writing for as long as I can remember. When my father passed away and I took some time off from work, I kept writing my 650-word column for *Nature & Health* magazine. It helped me get through one of the hardest times in my life. No matter what is happening, writing has always been the one constant that's kept me going. Until it wasn't.

One of the reasons I stopped writing was because a manuscript wasn't getting the response I was hoping for. The book didn't work and no matter what I did I couldn't get it to work. In the end, I abandoned it and, believing writing to be the reason for this, I abandoned that as well. By abandoning writing, I abandoned myself.

Laistrygonians and Cyclops,
angry Poseidon—don't be afraid of them:
you'll never find things like that on your way
as long as you keep your thoughts raised high,
as long as a rare excitement
stirs your spirit and your body.

Writing helps me get my thoughts onto the page where I can see them in the daylight. When my thoughts are dark, an hour of writing lightens them. Anxiousness eases, loneliness subsides. Writing creates a rare excitement for no particular reason. It stirs my spirit and my body, bringing a sense of meaning and purpose. Writing can restore my inner peace in an instant while offering moments of pure, unadulterated joy. Yet I gave all this up because I thought I wasn't good enough.

Laistrygonians and Cyclops,
wild Poseidon—you won't encounter them
unless you bring them along inside your soul,
unless your soul sets them up in front of you.

But this is not why I write. I don't write because I want people to think I'm good. I write because of how it makes me feel, and writing makes me feel good. Writing gives me the tools to navigate my own life. It doesn't remove the obstacles or the discomfort; writing merely softens them. It makes the struggles bearable. Plus, when I'm writing, I never feel alone. I'm in the company of words and sentences and ideas that have a way of wrapping themselves around me like a loving hug. It's impossible to feel alone when I'm writing. I'm too busy feeling connected.

Maybe this is why the homeless man and woman didn't look up when I stood in front of them. They were already connected to something within themselves, within their own worlds. Not the hard, physical worlds, but the worlds they were making and creating with their instruments – an orange pencil, a guitar.

What would have happened if I had been writing on a regular basis? Would that night in February have played out the way it did? Would I have drunk that much alcohol? Would I have felt swallowed up by loneliness when the car door closed behind me? Would I have come home and reached for the bottle of eye make-up remover instead of the pills? I'll never know. The only thing I do know is that these questions and all the other questions I have about life and what I'm doing here don't arise when I'm writing on a regular basis. There's no reason for them to.

Hope the voyage is a long one.
May there be many a summer morning when,
with what pleasure, what joy,
you come into harbors seen for the first time;
may you stop at Phoenician trading stations
to buy fine things,
mother of pearl and coral, amber and ebony,
sensual perfume of every kind—
as many sensual perfumes as you can;
and may you visit many Egyptian cities
to gather stores of knowledge from their scholars.

I sit up, leaning back against the fabric-covered bedhead. I open Henri to a blank page and begin moving the pen across it. I'm not writing anything in particular. These words are not part of my daily quota. I'm simply writing because I now understand how important it is. It's nourishment for my soul.

Could it really be this easy? Could it be a case of simply picking up a pen or a paintbrush or a musical instrument and just making something? Could it be possible to overcome life's struggles by performing a skit or painting a wall or playing a tune on the piano? Can the act of making something give us the sense of connection and purpose we're all searching for? Is creativity how we can truly nourish the soul?

Keep Ithaka always in your mind.
Arriving there is what you are destined for.
But do not hurry the journey at all.
Better if it lasts for years,

so you are old by the time you reach the island,
wealthy with all you have gained on the way,
not expecting Ithaka to make you rich.

As I shower, I think about why we don't make more space in our lives to just create, for no other reason than the experience itself. We all have obligations and responsibilities we have to meet, some more than others. Yet we seem to have allowed it all to take over our lives, taking us further away from our creative instincts and inner callings. But then we become so overwhelmed, it feels like we're being suffocated by them, lost within them. We lose hope. We can't see a way out.

Ithaka gave you the marvellous journey.
Without her you would not have set out.
She has nothing left to give you now.

Creativity has the power to restore hope. It restored mine when I had none and it continues to do so throughout this process. My kind of creativity involves words; telling stories that are meaningful to me and hopefully to others. When I write, I become a better version of myself – someone who stops the car and walks up to movie stars having a snooze on the side of the freeway for a chat. For others, creativity might be something entirely different. It can be expressed in infinite forms. Whatever way that is, I know now that it has the potential to guide us back to ourselves by reconnecting us with our life force. Creativity *is* life force. It's the way back to life, back to who we truly are. Creativity is the other way home.

And if you find her poor, Ithaka won't have fooled you.
Wise as you will have become, so full of experience,
you will have understood by then what these Ithakas mean.

Insight of the Day

Pick up a pen or a paintbrush or an instrument. Make something. For no other reason than to remind yourself of who you are and why you're here. If you feel like it, share your creation with others. Or don't. Just keep creating.

Day 23

The never-ending story

Barry's has the look and feel of an old warehouse stripped to its original form – brick and exposed beams – before being transformed into an ultra-hip café. When I arrive, it's brimming with Sunday morning activity – young fashionistas and families mostly. The atmosphere is relaxed, except for the staff, who dart about wearing focused expressions. I slide into one of the empty tables in the centre of the café as a pretty blonde waitress appears with a pen and tiny notebook.

After placing my order, I pull out the Writers Festival program to remind myself of the sessions I've booked at the Northcote Town Hall, a short walk from the café. The first one is called *Extraordinary Routines* and it's a panel on the importance of creative routines. That's something I'm convinced is essential in a creative life and which I experienced on Day 8. Then again, who wants to think about routines on a Sunday morning?

When I wander into the hall half an hour later, I'm not surprised to find it almost empty. I count a total of fifteen people, including the three authors and host patiently waiting on stage. I choose one of the empty seats in the front row and one of the panellists – an attractive, well-dressed woman with shoulder-length dark hair – turns and smiles.

Clint Greagen is up first. He's the creator of a blog called *Reservoir Dad*. 'I write until about 11.30 pm,' he begins, 'then I retreat to the bedroom where I perform my husbandly duties of pleasuring my sexually insatiable wife.' The crowd laughs. He goes on to reveal that he 'may or may not wear pants' when he writes. Rather than take his word for it, he encourages us to try it ourselves. While it might not affect the quality of the work, it can potentially help to get the creative juices flowing, so to speak.

Clint's a married father of four. He's also been writing every day of his life since he was eighteen. Even with the pressures and responsibilities of raising a young family, he hasn't missed a day of writing. Despite the late nights, he gets up every day at 5.00 am, admitting, 'I know I'll feel better at having lost an hour of sleep and having written.' Wrapping up his presentation, he offers some parting words, 'Start writing. Keep writing. Don't ever stop writing.'

Start writing. Keep writing. Don't ever stop writing.

'Our next speaker is one of Australia's bestselling romance fiction writers,' says the host. 'She's written over thirty books and is just about to release her latest, *The Perfumer's Secret*. Would you please welcome to the podium the wonderful Fiona McIntosh.'

The woman I shared a smile with earlier stands up and strides across the stage. There's something about her that is immediately captivating. Of course, it could be the fact that she's written thirty books, a number I find inspiring, if not incomprehensible. But there's more to it. I open Henri to a new page, my pen poised.

'I'm not one of those people who grew up wanting to be a writer,'

Fiona tells us. 'It never occurred to me until I made the decision to become one. I'd been running a magazine with my husband, but with my fortieth birthday approaching I started wondering, "Is this it?" Everything in my life was going great – I had a loving husband, two wonderful boys, a successful career – but I wasn't satisfied. I wanted more. So I thought about what that might be and eventually decided on becoming a writer.'

I'm enthralled by Fiona's no-nonsense approach. It's different to my 'total nonsense, many excuses, all of them bullshit' approach. Fiona explains how she took on the task of becoming a writer as if she had chosen to become a doctor or lawyer or any other profession. 'I knew I had to first learn how to write. I did my research, found out who was the best writer in Australia at the time and signed up for Bryce Courtenay's week-long writers' retreat. I learnt everything I could about the craft. When I returned home I spent the next twelve months writing my first manuscript, which I then sold to HarperCollins. It never crossed my mind that I wouldn't.'

So what about self-doubt?

'I've never had it. When I decide to do something, I do it. There's no magic in it. It's hard work that makes people successful. Writing is a business and I treat it as such. I've got to make a living. No one is going to do that for me. No one will do your work for you. You are the only one who can do the work.'

Fiona is clearly a worker. But when she tells us she began writing at the age of forty, there's an audible gasp. She can't be a day over fifty. Doing the numbers in my head that would mean she averages three books a year. It's simply not possible. There's another gasp when she confirms she does in fact write three books a year and has done for the last ten years, adhering to a strict word count and schedule. 'I'm always writing one, editing another, and researching the third,' she explains. She writes four days a week and it takes her twelve weeks to write 120,000 words. This time I punch the numbers into my phone to calculate her daily word count. It's approximately 2500 words a day, which is only five hundred more than what I'm doing. The impossible still feels impossible, but a little less so.

By the end of the day, Henri is fat with quotes and insights. While the speakers' creative routines may vary, the message is the same: 'To be a writer you have to write on a regular basis and you have to keep writing.'

Start writing. Keep writing. Don't ever stop writing.

It's not just these authors sharing this message. Every speaker has said the same thing. These are people with partners and children and responsibilities. They have houses to clean, food to cook, kids to raise, public profiles to maintain, and events such as these to attend. Yet there is one thing they all have in common: they write *every day*. Some of them write early in the morning. Others late at night. Some write with their pants on. Some don't. But they all write. Every day. No matter what. And they keep writing. They never stop.

I ask the taxi driver to drop me a few blocks away from the hotel. I feel like strolling the streets for a while, soaking up the atmosphere of the city. It's been an exhilarating three days, and I'm feeling fulfilled and connected to something greater than myself. Being around other writers reminds me of who I am. Knowing this instils a sense of peace and calm, while simultaneously elevating my spirit. I understand the language spoken by these people, as well as the anxieties and jubilations. They are similar to my own experiences and it's a reminder that despite writing being a solitary act, I'm never alone in it. I feel a deep sense of belonging.

Standing on the corner of Spring and Bourke streets, the happy sounds of jazz fill the air. I notice three women brandishing instruments – a bass, an accordion and a trumpet – playing in unison, their bodies bouncing along to the upbeat rhythm of their tune. I smile. They're making their art and sharing it with the world, regardless of whether the world is paying attention. They can't see me watching them from across the street and don't know how much I'm enjoying their music. They play anyway.

With a few hours to spare before I'm due to fly back to Sydney, I take my laptop to the hotel bar where I plan on getting a start on my two thousand words. But the doors are closed and the bar is dark and empty. I head towards the hotel restaurant instead. Also closed. Through the glass doors I can see frantic activity: crisp white table cloths are being thrown over tables, cutlery is being polished and placed in position while elaborate chandeliers hanging overhead are dimmed. It's almost six o'clock and the dinner crowd will soon be arriving. I knock on the glass door and a woman dressed in a black and white uniform unlocks it and greets me with a professional smile.

'Is there any chance I could just sit quietly somewhere and write?' I ask.

'Of course,' she says. 'Just as long as you don't mind us setting up around you.'

'Not at all. Thank you.'

I'm offered a seat on one of the cream lounges lining the wall of the historic dining room. Copper fans spin lazily overhead even though it's fifteen degrees outside. I marvel at the ornate ceilings and the tall, polished wooden columns. Regal curtains frame the large windows that look out across to Parliament House. Ella Fitzgerald's easy voice fills the room. I feel like a privileged guest in someone's grand yet welcoming home.

A well-dressed elderly man and his wife are the first of the dinner crowd to arrive, shuffling their way into the lounge area. The man looks like he's in his eighties. Possibly even nineties. They order drinks and sit down quietly together. I stop typing. There are stories behind the lines and creases on their faces but they are silent now. I wonder what they think about as they sit, slowly sipping their drinks. Eventually, I start typing again.

A few minutes later a waiter appears, telling the couple their table is ready. The gentleman stands and turns towards me. 'The ghosts of this place wouldn't believe what you're doing in this room right now,' he says.

I stop typing and look up, slightly taken back by the strange comment. 'I'm not sure what you mean,' I say.

'This is not a place for that,' he says abruptly, pointing towards my computer.

I give a respectful nod. He's probably right, but when you've committed to a daily creative practice, sometimes concessions have to be made, even if there are some who don't approve or agree. As a writer, my job is to write anyway.

Insight of the Day

Start writing. Keep writing. Don't ever stop writing. Or whatever else it is you love doing. Do it every day, if possible. If others don't approve, start doing it, keep doing it and don't ever stop doing it.

Day 24

No more excuses

My return home from Melbourne has been met with a depressing thud. This is not surprising. After being on such a creative high for the past three days there was only one direction for my mood to go upon re-entering the world of the regular and the mundane. Yet at the same time I know that back home is where I need to be. There's only so much listening to other people you can do before it stops feeling productive and starts to look and feel a lot more like procrastination.

It was Fiona McIntosh who said, 'If you're a writer, there's no excuse not to write.' Of course, this is not true. There are many of excuses not to write. I can come up with at least ten of them right now:

1. I don't want to write.
2. I've been writing every day. I need a break.
3. The dishwasher needs unpacking.
4. The dishwasher needs packing.

5. It's a lovely day outside. I should be making the most of it.

6. It's a terrible day outside, I should be [insert any activity other than writing].

7. I have to unpack my bags.

8. I need money. I should look for a job.

9. I need to call [insert person's name].

10. I could use a nap.

I've got dozens more, all waiting to be unleashed at the first sign of discomfort. One of the fascinating parts of this process has been watching the excuses appear yet not allowing myself to be seduced by them. Usually an excuse will surface and I'll respond with something like, 'You're right. It *is* a lovely day outside' or 'I am tired and I really could use that nap.' The thing is I really am tired. After all, it takes a lot of energy to ignore the constant barrage of excuses that keep popping up, energy that could have been put to much better use, such as writing.

Let's take the other day, for example. I was a few hundred words shy of my daily word count when I suddenly I felt sleepy. 'Just a few minutes,' I told myself as I headed towards the couch. 'Five minutes max.' The trouble is I don't take five-minute naps. If I lie down, I'm not doing it so I can immediately get back up again. If I go down, I'm going for Delta. Although on this occasion, despite the fatigue, I was able to recognise this is one of the many excuses designed to throw me off track and thwart my commitment. So, I ignored it and kept writing. It wasn't easy but I felt better as a result.

There are always going to be excuses to not do what we've committed to doing, especially when it has something to do with creativity. We live in a society that values plenty of activities ahead of creative expression. Our excuses, therefore, seem legitimate and justified. The electricity bill needs paying. The fridge needs filling. The car needs washing. The kids need bathing. The garden needs weeding. The carpet needs cleaning. The light bulb needs changing. I know, I've used all of them, except for the 'kids need bathing' one. Although even without kids, I probably would whip this one out if I didn't have so many others to choose.

Unlike professions where people can be replaced with a phone call, no one can replace the artist. No one can write our stories or paint our pictures or take our photographs. That's the thing about creativity: we all have it and only we can do it. But still we refuse. There are as many excuses not to be creative as there are stars in the sky, and yet our unique creative expression is not something we can outsource. If we want to reap the riches, we have to pick up a shovel and start digging.

I understand why we put off being creative. Often hours will go by and it feels like all I've written are pages of crap. Sometimes it's hard not to feel like you're wasting your life. It's taken me years to be okay spending the majority of my time writing, accepting that much of what I write isn't going to be any good. It doesn't always have to be good. Like any profession, there are going to be good days and bad days. We show up anyway because that's our job.

Life moves fast. The older we get, the faster it moves. Yesterday, I was twenty-four years old, sitting on the patio of my friend's beach house in Los Angeles, holding a beer in one hand and a future full of possibilities in the other. Except it wasn't yesterday. It was almost twenty years ago. It just *feels* like yesterday. It also feels like we have the rest of our lives ahead of us. We say, 'I'll do it tomorrow' until a year or ten have passed. And then we think, 'Well I guess it's too late now.' Of course, it's never too late. Until it *is* and there are no more tomorrows.

Today is the only day we can be certain about. I remind myself of this on a daily basis. I have to write today because I can't be one hundred per cent sure about tomorrow. It's likely that I'll be around to enjoy another tomorrow but I can't know for sure. When an excuse does arise, it will be so real and so convincing that sometimes I can't help but run with it. These days, however, I know how much harder it is to come back to writing after being away from it for a while. When you're writing every day, it's much easier to keep writing every day.

So, instead of focusing on all the reasons *not* to write, I'll create a list of excuses *to* write. *I write because ...*

I love writing. It's my passion.

I feel better about myself.

I feel better about my life.

I feel better about everything.

I'm happier.

I feel connected. I no longer feel alone.

I become kinder towards people. I'm more likely to smile at strangers.

I can't think of anything else I would rather be doing.

I have stories I want to share.

I made a commitment to writing and I want to follow through on that commitment.

I have fun when I'm writing.

I could go on but I'm suddenly feeling the urge to start writing. I haven't yet decided on my next project and the risk is without a follow-up idea I'll lose momentum. One missed day of writing is all it takes to fall out of step and into the swamp of excuses. Therefore, it's critical I have a project to jump to once this one is done. I create another list of possible book ideas.

Fiona McIntosh said, 'Writing is a business and I treat it as such. I've got to make a living. No one is going to do that for me.' When going into business, it's essential to have a plan. It's the same with writing. Writing a book is a big commitment, often twelve months or more in the making. It's worth taking the time to ensure the idea is one I'm willing to remain committed to. In other words, an idea I'm going to 'stick to' once I've made my mind up.

I've never been much of a planner, believing planning and structure equalled limitation and restriction. When I began writing my first book, I started and just kept going. The first draft was a mess and took several years to clean up. Since then I've changed my tune about planning. Now, I *love* to plan. Planning is my friend. These days, I wouldn't contemplate writing a book without first writing a plan. Planning isn't about eliminating mystery or spontaneity; it's about creating a container in which mystery and spontaneity can unfold.

Choosing an idea for a book requires careful consideration. It's a bit like relationships. You want to make sure you really know someone before deciding to walk down the aisle. Otherwise, you'll find yourself spending a lot of time and money trying to get out of a situation you didn't want to be in in the first place. The same goes for writing a book. My inability to stick to an idea wasn't because I lack discipline or commitment: it's because I wasn't sure about the idea; I didn't take the time to get to know it; I didn't *plan*.

As a result, my confidence suffered. By jumping from one thing to the next while struggling to commit, I began believing I didn't have what it took. But this was wrong. I *did* have the discipline and I *was* committed. I just had to sit down and figure out where best to focus that discipline and commitment. Not all ideas are great ideas. Planning helps to work this out.

With this in mind, I'm determined to do things differently. Rather than jumping into bed with any old idea, I'm going to do some planning first. I have a few story ideas in my head, some which have emerged over the past few weeks while others have been hanging around for years. Having written a list, I'm able to narrow my ideas down to only those that truly excite me. I'm going to spend some time 'dating' each idea before making the decision to commit. I do this by writing a few thousand words, fleshing out the story and identifying whether there is one. If I'm still excited at the end of this process, then the idea has potential. If not, then I've only invested a few thousand words. Better to break up with the idea now before finding yourself fifty thousand words in and pining after that 'other' tale you had your eye on.

I'm over most of my ideas within the first couple of paragraphs. This process has saved me many hours and much heartache. Yet there's one idea I keep coming back to. I've never written romance fiction before, or any fiction. I have no idea how to do it which is why it's the perfect idea. You don't know until you give it a go.

With the next book idea decided, I break it into smaller parts. Starting a new book can be daunting, made even more so if approached in one big chunk of writing. The thought of starting an eighty-thousand-word book – the average word count for a romantic fiction novel – is enough to inspire a wave of excuses. Planning takes the impossible and turns it into the possible, reducing the risk of distraction, procrastination or avoidance.

'Doing the numbers' is one of my favourite parts of the planning phase. Let's say I'm committed to writing two thousand words a day, every day. For an eighty-thousand-word book, that's ...

80,000 words / 2000 words = 40 days

40 days / 7 days per week = 6 weeks

That's a first draft in six weeks!

Maybe I'm not prepared to work that hard. Two thousand words a day is a lot. What if I gave myself three months? That works out to be approximately nine hundred and fifty-two words a day, which is more manageable. Three months to write an eighty-thousand-word novel. It takes longer for me to lodge my tax return.

Insight of the Day

Make a list of reasons to write and then make a plan to get on with it.

Day 25

Inspire yourself

'Hey! How was Melbourne?' asks Emma as I stroll into the café. She's peering over the headline of the latest budget cut, squinting in the light of the morning sun. Ava is sitting at another table with Earl, attempting to stab a single poached egg with a knife.

'Amazing,' I say, pulling out the empty seat opposite. I give her a quick rundown.

'Well, Brett and I have been so inspired by your writing challenge, we've decided we're going to do our own creative challenge.'

'That's awesome! Are you going to write a book together?'

Emma glances around the café before leaning in. 'No. We've committed to having sex every day for the month of September.'

'That is so not what I was expecting,' I say, laughing. 'But I love it. You can call it Sexy September.'

'Sex is a form of creativity. Plus, we've both been so exhausted lately, especially with Ava, neither of us can be bothered. It's not good for our relationship.'

'It's a great idea.'

'Perhaps you can be our coach and help us stay accountable?'

'Sure,' I say, remembering my conversation with the shop assistant from Fine & Sonny and the importance of being accountable to someone. 'Actually, the idea of me checking up to make sure you and Brett are having sex every day does sound slightly creepy. I think you're on your own with this one.'

Emma laughs. 'No! You have to help us stay motivated.'

'I don't think you're going to need any help staying motivated!'

'Are you kidding? We have a baby!'

Brett emerges from the bathroom. 'So I hear you're gearing up for an exciting September?' I say with a wink.

Brett looks confused. 'What's happening in September?'

'You *know* ...' says Emma.

Brett shrugs his shoulders before Emma leans in and whispers in his ear. 'Oh that,' he says, rolling his eyes and opening up the paper.

'Don't make out as if it wasn't *your* idea,' I say with a grin.

'It wasn't,' he says. 'This was definitely her idea.'

Emma turns to me. 'Actually, this was your idea.'

'Mine? How is this my idea? You're the ones who've adulterated my creative pilgrimage. Although I do approve. I'm also jealous.'

'Come on, honey. It will be great for our relationship.' Emma snuggles into Brett who is now immersed in the newspaper. He suddenly looks up as if struck by an idea.

'If one person is tired and wants to go to sleep, the other person can have sex with themselves?'

'Masturbation doesn't count,' I say. 'Although ideally the creative pilgrimage is something to do on your own, so perhaps it should.'

'I wasn't talking about me,' says Brett, laughing. 'I'll be the one asleep.'

'Come on, babe,' says Emma. 'It'll be good for us.'

Brett flicks his newspaper to the next page and I take that first glorious sip of caffeine. I love the idea of others getting into the spirit of my commitment. Emma and Brett's has reinforced my own. It feels like the extra encouragement I need to keep going, even though I'm not as worried as I was at the beginning about giving up. Now I'm afraid something is going to happen that would force me to quit. I'm therefore still slightly on edge and taking each day one at a time.

Rhett strolls into the café just as Emma and Brett are saying their farewells. He looks tired and unshaven as if he's had a rough night. 'Hey, how's Sophie?' I ask. 'I haven't seen her in a while.'

'She's great, busy with work so I haven't seen her either.'

'But you're all good?'

Rhett nods. 'I hope so.'

'Did something happen?'

Rhett hesitates. 'Well, we took a drive up the coast on the weekend and we got talking ... about you.'

'Me? Why me?'

'We were talking about your creative pilgrimage I mentioned how I thought it was inspiring and it's helped me get back to working on my script again.'

'That's kind of you to say. So what's the problem?'

'Eventually she admitted it made her jealous.'

'Why? She has no reason to be jealous.'

'I don't know.'

'It sounds like she wants to know she inspires you.'

'She does. She is one of the kindest people I've ever met. She's so loving and considerate. She's not afraid to take risks and go on adventures. I mean I *love* being with her.'

I offer a smile. 'Have you told her this?'

'I tell her all the time.' Rhett pauses. 'Okay, well, not *all* the time.

But I do tell her. I think. I'm not sure. I might not use those exact words.'

'Instead, you tell her that I inspire you, the girl from the café who you occasionally hang out with. Good one.'

Rhett smiles. 'I see your point.'

'Sometimes I wonder if I'm wasting my time with this project but then I hear how it's affecting the people around me and it helps me to keep going. Emma and Brett have just committed to having sex every day in September.'

Rhett laughs. 'Really?'

I nod. 'I probably shouldn't have told you that. I think it was shared in confidence. But the point is, we all inspire each other.'

'I know what you mean. I remember this guy coming up to me in a bar. He'd seen me in a movie and said that something my character had said made him realise what he needed to do to save his marriage. That was pretty cool.'

'That's amazing. See, we all want to know we're making a difference. When someone tells me that they've enjoyed something I've written, it makes my day. I know it shouldn't matter, but it does. It feels good and it inspires me to write more.'

'It's true. After that guy came up to me, it made me want to do an even better job in the next role I played. I remember pushing myself more than usual.'

'I've got to run. There are words waiting to be written. Tell Sophie how she inspires you.'

Rhett nods, 'I will.'

On my walk home, the morning's conversations make me consider how well I communicate to those I care about and the impact they have on me creatively. When I meet Grace at the theatre later that night I realise I've never seen her perform, even though she's been on TV and stage and even won a national award for her acting. She's one of my best friends but how can I tell her she inspires me if I've never made the effort to see her in her element?

'Hey, Grace?' I ask, as we're standing in line at the bar waiting to order a couple of glasses of wine.

'Yeah?'

'So you know how I've never seen you act in anything?'

'Even though I've read all your books and am clearly a much better friend? Yes.'

'Okay, well, it's time to change that. Have you got any recordings I can watch? Like a showreel or something?'

'You don't have to do that.'

'Yes I do. You've read all my books and I am a terrible friend for not having made an effort. Plus, I want to.'

Grace eyes me suspiciously for a moment before saying, 'I'd love that. I've got a few tapes at home.'

'As in *video*tapes?'

Grace rolls her eyes. 'DVDs. I'm not that much older than you.'

'Great. I can't wait!'

'So where did all this come from?' she asks.

I tell her about the conversations I had at the café earlier. 'Acting is such a big part of who you are. I know how much it means to you and you mean a lot to me. I want to see that side of you. I'm sorry I haven't asked until now.'

'Well, thanks, Heds. That's very sweet of you.'

'Plus, I still want you to read my books!'

'Ha! So that's it. I will always read your books.'

'Thanks, Grace. You're a good friend.'

She smiles, throwing an arm around my shoulder adding, 'Yes, I am.' She turns back towards the line of people standing in line, waiting to get a drink. 'Now, what's taking so long?'

Insight of the Day

Tell people when they inspire you. Say it to their face. 'You inspire me.' Write them a card. Send them a pigeon. Let them know. Chances are you'll make their day.

Day 26

A glorious luxury

I decide to start Day 26 differently. I'll go to Smith's instead of Earl's! As I pull up at the lights near Centennial Park, the car behind toots its horn. I peer into the rear-view mirror, about to glare at the driver behind when, instead of an angry face glaring back, I see Emma. She's waving from behind the wheel. She pulls alongside my passenger window. 'Hey!' she calls out. 'Funny meeting you here.'

'I was just thinking about how I miss seeing all of you this morning.'

'And here I am.'

'And here you are. Not heading to the café either?'

Emma shakes her head. 'I thought I'd change it up today. I'm taking Ava to Grandma's so I'll grab a coffee on the way.'

Ava is strapped into her baby seat and peering curiously at me. I smile and wave. She continues peering curiously.

The light turns green and we continue along Anzac Parade before drawing to a stop at another set of red lights. 'So when am I going to be able to read this thing?' Emma calls out.

'I don't know. I don't know if anyone is going to read it. I'm just focused on finishing it. Hey, that reminds me. How's Sexy September going?'

Emma smirks as the light turns green once more. I laugh, and she waves as we veer off in different directions. I smile as I continue towards my destination, grateful for the little touch of magic.

—

Ten minutes later I'm at Smith's. It's surprisingly calm for this time of the morning. Matt, the owner, is standing behind the coffee machine. His eyes flick up and he nods. 'Long time no see. What's happening?'

'Hopefully a long black,' I say, dropping some coins on the counter. 'You look well. How are you?'

'Fantastic,' he says. 'And you? What have you been up to?'

'The usual. Writing every day.'

Matt nods. 'Well, exercise is always good for the brain.'

Huh? 'I can't say I've done much of that to be honest. I walk to Clovelly every once in a while.'

Matt glances up, eyebrows furrowed. 'Didn't you just say you were riding every day?'

'*Riding?*' I say with a laugh. 'No! I said I've been *writing* every day.'

'Oh. I can't say I took you for a bike rider.'

'I can't say I would either.'

'So what are you *writing*?'

I tell him about the creative pilgrimage, which is now only days away from completion.

'There's no way I could do that,' he says.

'Of course you could. It's probably just not your thing.'

'What have you got out of it?'

'Lots! It's giving me my confidence back. I'm more engaged in the world. But the biggest thing is knowing I have what it takes to commit to something and stick to it.'

'Todd! Cappuccino!' Matt yells, before returning his attention to me. 'Great things happen when you commit to something and stick to it. That's how I approach my business. But you have to be passionate about what you're doing, otherwise you'll never get through the tough times. And there are always tough times.'

'Always,' I agree.

'Nothing good comes without a little sacrifice.'

Sacrifice. Another one of the words which first appeared in black paint on the walking path in the first week. Matt slides my beloved coffee over the bench. 'Enjoy.'

'Thanks. I will. This is one thing I won't be giving up.'

Wandering slowly around the corner towards Anna's office, I think how sacrifice relates to creativity. It's a word I often bump up against, possibly because it means giving something up, usually something you enjoy, to achieve something else. Let's take sleep, for example. I recall several of the authors at the Writers Festival talking about how they would sacrifice an extra hour of sleep in exchange for an extra hour of writing. I love sleeping and writing in equal measure. Why do I have to choose between one or the other? For me, it's an impossible choice.

Like ambition, sacrifice requires further investigation and so when I arrive at the office, I look it up. The traditional religious definitions aren't doing it for me. My least favourite definition, however, is perhaps the most common one: 'an act of giving up something valued for the sake of something else regarded as more important or worthy'. *Why does it have to be this way? Isn't it possible to have it all?*

Language evolves over time. Definitions change and adapt depending on the era. My mother used to love the word 'gay', which in her youth meant a light and carefree disposition or something brightly coloured. These days, as we all know, 'gay' is the casual term for homosexuality. While Mum has nothing against homosexuality, for a while she refused to surrender the word to its new meaning. Eventually I had to insist that it was no longer appropriate to call someone 'gay' because of their sunny disposition. The definition was correct but the use had changed. Reluctantly, she conceded.

Investigating further, I find that the word 'sacrifice' originates from the Latin word *sacrificium* which is related to *sacrificus* 'sacrificial'. This term is derived from *sacer* 'holy, sacred' and *facere*, meaning 'to make' or 'to do'. It's a linguistic maze, yet by stripping back the word to its original form, it's clear just how much the meaning has changed throughout the centuries and how far we have strayed from these origins. Originally, the word 'sacrifice' simply meant to make something sacred or holy.

This is a definition I can get behind. But how did the word come to have so much negativity associated with it?

Religion played a big part. Christianity and the crucifixion of Christ were considered the ultimate 'sacrifice'. The Church claimed the term, redefining it to serve its own interests. Using the image of Jesus nailed to the cross, the Church created an association of suffering to instil fear in the masses from which it promised salvation, thereby creating a dependency. Instead of 'giving up' something to God, you gave it up to the Church instead, usually in the form of time, money and freedom.

The original definition of 'sacrifice' offers a whole new meaning and, for me, a new relationship with the concept. I've often recoiled when hearing the phrase 'you have to make sacrifices in life', implying this idea of suffering and the giving up of something enjoyable, an idea that doesn't inspire me to start making sacrifices. Yet making something sacred by turning it over to a higher power is a different experience. Suffering becomes something we sacrifice rather than sacrifice being an act of suffering.

The mind is responsible for creating much of our suffering, especially the mind of a creative person. Fear, insecurity, procrastination, self-consciousness, doubt, worry, anxiety, jealousy, laziness. Imagine if we could *sacrifice* these states of mind simply by making them sacred. That is, to hand them over to God, or a power greater than ourselves. By giving our suffering to God, we make it holy; we make it sacred. Our suffering becomes our offering and in giving it away, we no longer have to endure it alone.

—

Later that evening, feeling lighter from all the suffering I've sacrificed, I head north across the Harbour Bridge for a book launch in McMahon's Point. The book is *The Truth According To Us* by Annie Barrows. Annie famously wrote *The Guernsey Literary and Potato Peel Pie Society* with her aunt, Mary Ann Shaffer.

She's a petite woman from San Francisco with a lot of energy and confidence. She begins her talk by telling us about her aunt, Mary Ann. 'She had always dreamt of writing something that someone would like enough to want to publish. Finally, after writing her whole life, her dream was set to come true. A publisher picked up the manuscript that would eventually become *The Guernsey Literary and Potato Peel Pie Society*, although there were significant changes that needed to be made. Unfortunately, Mary Ann fell ill, so she asked if I would be willing to finish the book for her. She had done an incredible job with it, but it needed significant rewriting. The book was published four months after she died. It kills me that she didn't get to see so many people enjoy it.'

Annie was already an author in her own right when she took on the job of rewriting her aunt's manuscript. She had a Masters of Fine Arts in Creative Writing and was the creator of the children's book series, *Ivy and Bean*. *The Guernsey Literary and Potato Peel Pie Society* became an international bestseller and gave a lot of pleasure to many people around the world. But I can't help dwelling on the fact that her aunt never got to revel in the success. Her dream was to be a published author but she spent her whole life believing her work wasn't good enough. To die months before her dream was realised is tragic. I couldn't imagine it. Except I can imagine it. Very clearly. I have the same dream and the same fear. The main reason I decided to self-publish was that I didn't want the publishing houses to reject me, which I was sure they would. I literally bypassed the rejection stage.

Annie moves on to discuss her latest book, *The Truth According To Us*. It's a story set in the summer of 1938 about Layla, a young woman who is assigned to cover the history of a small town in West Virginia. Nothing much appears to happen in this town until she's invited into the home of an unconventional family. Layla discovers that beneath the quiet veneer are untold secrets. When Annie finishes, she opens the floor to questions. A middle-aged woman at the back of the room puts her hand up.

'Thank you for sharing those wonderful insights to your book, Annie,' says the woman. 'What I enjoyed most were the conversations between the characters. You capture the dialogue with such authenticity; I was wondering, how did you do this? Did you listen in on people's conversations and take notes?'

Annie laughs. 'No, I didn't eavesdrop. Although I did for the *Ivy and Bean* series because kids say the most brilliant things that you just can't make up, even if you wanted to. Adults can have a hard time capturing the naivety and innocence of children, so I did eavesdrop then, but not with this book.

'The way I see it, dialogue is a form of *translating*. When you write dialogue, you are translating reality, and to write good dialogue, you're attempting to create the *effect* of being real without it being real. Imagine if you listened to someone's conversation and then put it down on paper word for word, it wouldn't be very interesting to read. Writing dialogue is a delicate art because it's not a real life conversation, but as a writer, you have to produce the effect that it is. So I'm glad that it worked and it had that effect on you. That was my aim.'

I have never heard the writing of dialogue described so succinctly and I pull out Henri and start taking notes. Annie asks for another question. My hand shoots up. 'Yes,' she says, turning to me with a smile.

'This is a large book and I imagine it would have taken you some time to write. I'm wondering whether you follow any kind of daily routine?'

Annie smiles. 'When my kids were little my routine was very different. Back then it was pretty crazy. I would be running around trying to get everything organised so I could steal myself away for a window of writing time. Back then I'd have to grab whatever time I could. Then when I got it, I'd be sitting down at my computer ready to write and I would hear my kids breathing at the door. Sometimes I would be in the middle of a sentence when I would have to stop and go and be with them. So it was a lot harder then to stick to any kind of routine.

'But my kids are older now and they're no longer breathing through the door, so for the last five years or so I've had the glorious pleasure of being able to write all day for as long as I want. And often, I do. I'll sit down at my desk at 9.30 am and keep writing until I fall over. It's not really a routine because when you love doing something so much you just do it.' A smile stretches across Annie's face as her eyes light up. 'You know, it's a glorious, *glorious* luxury to be able to write every day.'

I feel a smile stretch across my own face. I do know. It is a glorious luxury.

This might be why I've been splashing around in a puddle of guilt lately. It's as though by not working in an office, I'm not working. Or that by that by doing something I love it's somehow selfish and self-indulgent and possibly even *deluded.* Today was one of my least productive days despite sitting in an office. Over the past twenty-six days, I've worked harder and longer than I have in a long time. I've worked in cafés, at the beach, at the park and on my couch. Yet I feel guilty because I've enjoyed the work and the environments in which I've done it. Annie summed it up perfectly. My work is a luxury, a 'glorious, glorious luxury'. There's nothing to feel guilty about, so what if I didn't? It's certainly not serving me or my work in any way. What if I sacrificed guilt?

Insight of the Day

Sacrifice suffering. You don't need it. It's not serving you. So, give it up. Hand it over to a Higher Source, a Greater Power, a Whatever-You-Want-To-Call-It. Then get back to work.

Day 27

Prepare yourself

It's 8.43 am and I press my hand hard against my chest as I cough. A searing pain rips through my torso like a knife. Sometime during the night, I seem to have contracted a chest infection, although not the kind that creeps up on you slowly with a sore throat or a headache. Not the kind that gives you at least a day's warning. The infection has hijacked my body – and my mind.

What are you doing? This is stupid. You've just wasted an entire month.

My chest burns as I stare at the 536 words on the screen, willing the 537th to come. It doesn't. More worryingly, I don't care. I'm overwhelmed with negative thoughts and I don't have the energy to fight back. This state of mind has the potential to derail the pilgrimage. And while I might not care now, I would care very much once the month is over.

Suddenly, words spoken by my Year 12 art teacher, Mrs Brown, ring through my head like a school bell at lunchtime. 'There's nothing of interest here,' the voice hisses. 'Your work is trite, Hedley. Trite!'

I didn't know what the word 'trite' meant. The tone of disgust suggested it wasn't complimentary. Six months into my final year, Mrs Brown had taken over from Mr Byrne, my art teacher of four years and one of my all-time favourites. Whereas Mr Byrne had always been kind, encouraging and supportive, Mrs Brown took an instant dislike to me and was not averse to making these feelings known, not just to me, but to the whole class.

I was devastated when she took over. Although not as devastated as I was when she leaned over and hissed in my ear. Trite, I later discovered, means 'lacking originality or freshness; dull on account of overuse', not the words you want your new art teacher using to describe something you've invested six months in creating. In front of the whole class, she told me she would not be submitting my artwork to the school board for marking in its current state. She then handed me a bottle of white paint and, despite my protestations, instructed me to pour the paint over my almost-finished artwork and start again.

Author Brené Brown calls these sorts of incidents 'art scars'. We all have them. They're creative wounds born of the criticisms made about something we've made. Art scars cut deep and hang around. To slander a person's creativity is to slander their soul. Our vulnerability has been mocked and disparaged, and this is hard to recover from. Some people never do, especially if it happened at a young and impressionable age. They put down their pen or paintbrush and never pick it up again. While I've picked up a paintbrush once or twice over the years, it's rarely and never for very long. A part of me never entirely recovered from Mrs Brown's comments. Her words still return during times when I'm feeling vulnerable. Times like now.

A physical infection is almost always followed by mental infection. That is, a breakdown in rational thought. When I'm physically ill, I'm most at risk to succumbing to my art scars. My thoughts will turn on my creativity by morphing into the words of Mrs Brown. When my immune system is low, I don't have the energy to fight back. Instead, I'll ask questions like, 'What if she was right? What if my work is trite? What if it does suck? What if I'm not any good and I'm just kidding myself?'

As Mrs Brown's words circle my mind like a hungry vulture waiting to strike, a gentle and soothing voice suddenly swoops in and interrupts the negativity: *You're just tired. You're not feeling well. Don't believe what your thoughts are telling you. Don't listen to them and don't believe them (except these ones of course!). Just keep writing. Get the words done. That's all you have to do.*

The break in the negativity doesn't last long. Every cough emboldens the negative thoughts which return like a cyclone gathering speed. Although this time my thoughts spin around to something an author said during a Writers Festival session back in Melbourne. It was a panel discussion on the topic of becoming a professional writer. The host had asked the two authors on stage, 'So what advice would you offer those wishing to make writing their career?'

One of the authors, with an impressive list of career achievements, turned to the audience and said, 'If you want to be a writer and you want writing to be your profession, then prepare for poverty. Prepare to be poor.'

Prepare for poverty. Prepare to be poor.

I was enjoying listening to this author up to this point. He was intelligent, well-read and well-versed in the arts. When he offered this piece of well-intentioned advice, my pen stopped moving. I wasn't about to scribble these words down. These were not words I wished to remember. Although clearly I did remember them because suddenly these words are all I can think of.

Prepare for poverty. Prepare to be poor.

The words bounce around in my head like a tennis ball being thrown against a brick wall. I try to tell myself these were words spoken by a guy wearing a faded T-shirt and jeans with hunched shoulders and lines of disappointment etched into his face. Everything about him communicated defeat and the multiple ways in which writing had failed him, despite his several books and impressive Twitter following. His message of 'hope' was therefore about saving his audience from the same fate to which he had succumbed.

Prepare for poverty! Prepare to be poor!

I'm sure his intentions were genuine and that he was simply trying to prevent us from experiencing the pain and heartache he had endured. It's hard pursuing a creative passion as a professional career. But at least encourage us to figure this out for ourselves or suggest that perhaps it will be different. What's the point of giving advice if it's only going to play upon people's insecurities? We're already brilliant at talking ourselves out of our creative urges, we don't need help from others.

In a culture that values certainty, security and predictability, it takes courage to stand up and declare yourself an artist, especially a professional one. The response is often, 'And you can make money doing that?' Or, 'So what will you fall back on if (when) that doesn't work?' Of course, these aren't really questions but underlying judgments designed to talk you out of it and convince you to get back to your 'real' job.

Prepare for poverty! Prepare to be poor!

The young, nimble minds in the audience listened intently. They were taking his words and making them their own, turning them into ideas and beliefs that might eventually create realities. Not new realities but realities similar to what this author was warning us about. After enough years had passed and enough dreams had been shattered, these young authors would become old authors, throwing on that tired, old T-shirt and those decade-old jeans while muttering, 'Well, I guess that guy was right. Perhaps I should have listened. Maybe I should have prepared for poverty. After all, I'm broke.'

They'd make appearances at writers festivals and share their wisdom with the next generation of artists. 'This is just how it is, kids,' they'd say. 'Prepare for poverty. Prepare to be poor. This is what I was told and this is what I'm telling you. Don't make the same mistakes I did. Give up now while you still have a chance to make something of yourself.'

Prepare for poverty! Prepare to be poor!

There are countless successful authors who earn an income from doing what they love. Elizabeth Gilbert. Cheryl Strayed. Lena Dunham. Fiona McIntosh. Annie Barrows. These are a few names which come to mind, women who have worked hard on their craft, year after year, and who are rewarded for their labour. These are women who write regardless of their success. They write because it's their job. This is what they do.

Writing is my job and it's what I do too.

I wonder what I would say if I were one of these authors on stage. What advice would I offer? What message would I want to share? What kind of tone would I take? Would it be cautionary or inspirational? I hope it's the latter. I'd want people to know it's okay to be an artist if that's what you want to be. It's okay to follow the callings of your heart and do what you love. And it's even okay to make a living from it. You can do what you love and support your family at the same time. People have been doing this for centuries and will continue to do so. But you have to choose it. It's not going to be easy but neither is working in a job you hate. Once you've made a choice to walk the path of an artist, you then have to *prepare yourself*. But not for poverty.

To prepare for something is to act with intent. Our thoughts and actions put into motion what we believe we are about to experience. So, why prepare for poverty unless you have a genuine desire to be poor? On the other hand, if you want to experience success, prepare to be successful. If you want to experience wealth, prepare to be wealthy. If you want to experience happiness, prepare to be happy. If you want to experience public acclaim, prepare to be publicly acclaimed. If you want to experience inspiration, prepare to be inspired. If you want to experience a captivated audience, prepare to be captivating. If you want to experience a life where you get to do what you love every single day, prepare to live the life where you get to do what you love every single day.

Anyone can do this. No matter what you want to experience, you have to prepare for it. Prepare for what it is you want and then get back to work. Always come back to the work. But never prepare for what you don't want to experience. Never prepare for poverty and being poor, unless that's what you want.

Also, while you're preparing for everything that's coming your way, make friends with everything that *isn't*. Prepare to have it all but make friends with having nothing. Preparation then becomes *effective* preparation.

Prepare for success but make friends with failure.

Prepare for acclaim but make friends with criticism.

Prepare for acceptance but make friends with rejection.

Prepare for ease but make friends with struggle.

Prepare for enjoyment but make friends with frustration.

Prepare for excitement but make friends with disappointment.

Prepare for wonder but make friends with boredom.

Prepare for acclaim but make friends with anonymity.

Prepare for greatness but make friends with the ordinary.

Prepare for the best but make friends with the worst. Then get on with the job of making whatever it is you're making.

Never apologise for your creations. If someone doesn't like what you make, develop your craft. Polish it, amplify it, stretch it, expand and elevate it, but don't apologise for it. You're an artist. Art isn't perfect and nor should it be. You have nothing to apologise for.

And I'd finish with this: whatever you do, don't take my word for it! Never take anyone else's word for it, especially someone on stage. Be wary of those people. Go out into the world and figure it out for yourself. Create your own experiences. Learn from them and then come up with your own theories. If you feel so inclined, share those theories with others, but only as a way of offering to help or guide others towards their own experiences. Never take someone else's experience as your truth and never fall into believing your experience is the truth for others. Simply use it as a way to move yourself and others forward. We are all here to find our own way. We are all on our way home.

Having finished my imaginary speech, I've gone from flat on my back to perched up in bed with my computer resting on my lap. Those 537 words have somehow multiplied into well over two thousand. I have no idea where they came from; I'm only grateful that they came.

Insight of the Day

Prepare for what it is you want to experience. Make friends with what you don't. Never take anyone else's word for something. Let them be an invitation to figure it out for yourself. Put theories to the test. Challenge them. Debunk them. Make up your own theories and then give them to others to debunk.

Day 28

Winning the battle

It's midday when I poke my head out from under the covers through a sea of tissues. Yesterday's cough has grown into a complete physical smackdown. The virus has wrapped itself around my entire body and taken it hostage. I crash to the floor where I crawl on my hands and knees to the bathroom. It's not quite the celebratory finale to my creative pilgrimage I had envisioned. By the time I reach my destination, I'm exhausted and have to rest on the cold tiles. *How am I going to get two thousand words down when I can barely get to the bathroom?*

I wonder if the illness has anything to do with the conversation I had with Grace a couple of nights ago. We were standing outside the Sydney Opera House at intermission and Grace was telling me how Jimmy, her radiologist husband, had asked her to go to India where he was speaking at a conference. Grace didn't want to go, and I understood why.

'I got sooooooo sick when I went there with Anna!' I cried, rolling my head around in circles.

I invested so much energy telling her the story of getting sick in India I wonder if I somehow willed this new chest infection into existence. Words, both written and spoken, create and recreate our realities. I'll be writing about something or someone and within a day, or even just a few hours, that person will show up, or that situation will play out. It happens all the time. At one point, it was happening so often I began to feel afraid. The lines between life and art were becoming blurred. I didn't want the characters or scenes I was writing about to play out in real life. In Oscar Wilde's essay, *The Decay of Lying*, he famously wrote, 'Life imitates art far more than art imitates life.' Clearly life imitating art was more common than anyone thought.

In the seventh and final series of my favourite television series, *The West Wing*, Jimmy Smits plays the character of Matt Santos, a Mexican-American who's running to become the next US President. It was reported that *The West Wing* writer and producer, Eli Attie, based the character of Santos on the then junior Senator from Illinois, Barack Obama. Less than twelve months after the Matt Santos character became the fictional President of the TV series, Barack Obama announced he was running for President.

I don't know why or how this happens, only that it does. Perhaps it's because creative energy is the source of life. Much of what I write is inspired by my own experience. Therefore, I'm emotionally connected to what I'm writing, and I imbue my words with this emotion. Somehow the energy behind the words transforms them into actual events.

I'm no longer scared of this phenomenon, but I've learnt not to mess with it, either. It's made me more conscious of how I use words and what I choose to both write and talk about. I forget sometimes – such as during my recent conversation with Grace. I honestly don't know if it played any part in my current illness, but it's a distinct possibility.

Having survived the trip to the bathroom, I need some fresh air so I stagger down to the café for a coffee. I know caffeine isn't the recommended tonic for a chest infection, but if I don't give my system what it's become accustomed to I'll soon add unpleasant withdrawal symptoms to my list of woes. A thumping headache, on top of the other aches and pains, is the last thing I need. My phone rings on my way down the hill. I don't have the energy to talk to anyone but when I see it's Anna I change my mind.

'Hey,' I croak.

'Oh God, you sound awful,' she says.

'Uh-huh. What's happening?' I ask, keen to change the subject. 'How's your ankle?' Anna twisted her ankle the day before on a building site.

'Still sore. I think I might have sprained it. I'm walking slowly and just taking it one step at a time.'

'That sounds smart. I'll try that approach.'

'How's the writing going?'

'I'm struggling. I can barely move. I just have to get through these next few days and then I'm done.'

'One foot in front of the other.'

'Exactly.' I manage a smile. 'I know I'll feel better after I've done it. I just never expected it to be this hard.'

'You should be proud of yourself. What you've achieved is amazing.'

It's the small piece of encouragement I needed. If I'm going to get through these next few days and complete this challenge, I'm going to have to make some tough decisions. That is, I'm going to have to make some sacrifices. For starters, I'm going to ditch all social engagements for the rest of the month. I don't want to cancel the plans I've made, especially the plan to see my cousin perform in his new play at the Old Fitz, but if I don't, I'm compromising both my physical and mental health. My one and only commitment is to write two thousand words for the next three days.

But not going out raises another issue. For the past twenty-seven days, I've been inspired by what I've experienced within each twenty-four-hour period. No plans means no impromptu meetings with friends or conversations over coffee. Withdrawal from the world means instead of drawing inspiration from outside I'm going to have to draw it from within. Even if within is clogged with green phlegm.

—

Back home in bed, a book on my bookshelf with a shiny, silver cover catches my eye. I bought *The War of Art: Winning the Inner Creative Battle* by Steven Pressfield a few years ago when I was in Los Angeles. I remember devouring it at the time, finding it to be a brilliant and insightful read about the creative process and how to overcome the roadblocks that get in the way. I open the book to a random page. 'The professional endures adversity. He lets the birdshit splash down on his slicker, remembering that it comes clean with a heavy-duty hosing. He himself, his creative center, cannot be buried, even beneath a mountain of guano. His core is bulletproof. Nothing can touch it unless he lets it.'

Guano is the 'excrement of sea birds and cave-dwelling bats'. In other words, shit. It's an apt description for how I'm feeling. It's also a reminder that my creative centre is bulletproof. It can't be touched by anything, not unless I let it, which it's what I've been doing. I've been letting the shit overwhelm me by focusing on how sick I feel. I've been focused on how *hard* it is to write. Yet how can writing be hard if I'm not actually doing any? So what if all I write is shit (not that there are any shitty words!)? Surely it would be better to write shit instead of lying around all day feeling like it.

I grab Henri and open him to a fresh, new page.

Insight of the Day

There will be times when you feel like shit. Allow this to be your focus for a while but then stop. Change your perspective. Focus on something, anything, else. Withdraw from the world if you have to. Seek inspiration from within. Let the world introduce itself to you from behind closed doors.

Part V - Courage

From Latin *cor* meaning 'heart'.

'In one of its earliest forms, the word courage meant "To speak one's mind by telling all one's heart".' Brené Brown

Day 29

Creative alchemy

I push my toes into the sand, revelling in the promise of warmer weather on its way. It's Saturday morning and the beach is busy. Dropping my towel in front of the concrete wall and sitting down, I rest my head back and close my eyes. The sun's warmth brushes over my face and for a moment, I forget how atrocious I feel.

It's actually worse than yesterday. My head's become a mucous-making machine while my chest continues to rage against the slightest movement: a sniffle, a cough or even a deeper-than-normal breath. My stomach twists and turns as if contemplating expelling something but unable to make up its mind. It might be all the vitamins I swallowed earlier.

Opening my eyes, I see a man emerging from the surf with a rippled stomach that flexes with every step. As he walks his well-defined thighs up the beach, stopping to run a hand through his glistening mop of wet hair, my mouth falls open and stays open because I'm too tired to close it. He's a picture of perfection. As he bends down for a towel to dry his perfect face, I realise I know him. He owns the furniture store where I bought a bed and lounge a few years ago. I made several visits to his tastefully styled store, usually with Anna, and recall flirting with him. When he didn't flirt back, I decided he was gay.

But based on the very attractive, very pregnant blonde woman strolling up the beach behind him, I figure this may not be the case. Hot Furniture Man turns to his hot wife and hands her a towel, and as they cosy up together in blissful coupledom, I notice other young, attractive couples everywhere I look. Some are reading magazines; some are giggling. Some are sunbaking; some are stroking each other's bare skin. There are also several families scattered about, their children playing nearby. The scene is a reminder of everything I don't have but thought I would at this stage of my life. Suddenly, without warning, my mind is in free fall. I'd get up and leave except I don't have the energy. So I stay where I am as the dull ache of inadequacy sets in. It's easy to believe that you've failed at life while imagining everyone else's is better than yours. Especially so when you're sick and your face looks like a fruit bowl. But no good can come from playing the comparison game. I know because I've played it often and never won. There's always someone better, richer, younger, hotter, smarter, happier or luckier if you look hard enough. And rarely do you ever have to look that hard. The moment you find them is the moment you lose and, consequently, end up feeling like a loser.

'Did you hear Dad got knocked out by a cow?'

A family was sitting on the sand a few metres away in various states of recline, close enough for me to overhear their conversation. It's a welcome distraction. I'm curious to know how someone gets knocked out by a cow.

'Oh my God, Dad,' says one of the women. She's lying back,

resting her head in her hands. 'When did this happen?'

'About two weeks ago,' says a man in a raspy voice. I lean further over to my right. 'I was herding the cattle in and one of the buggers just stood there, looking at me. I was standing at the gate when he charged. Came at me full tilt. Next thing I knew –'

'He was out cold,' says another woman. She's older than the others and I assume she's the man's wife. 'I couldn't believe it. In all my years, I've never seen anything like it.'

The man has a ruggedly handsome face with grey hair sprouting from beneath a cream Akubra. He's wearing a light blue shirt tucked into a pair of cream jeans and a brown leather belt. On his feet, which are crossed over, are dark brown Blundstone boots adding to the 'from farm to beach' look.

'Oh Dad, that's awful. Are you alright?'

'Muuuuuuuuum!'

The conversation is interrupted by a scream so loud it feels like a hundred thousand pins stabbing my head. A kid wearing board shorts and a scowl slams a stick against the sand in front of me while directing the head-piercing scream at the family next to me. No one flinches. I want to punch him.

'Muuuuumuum!'

The scream turns into a bloodcurdling whine and I snap my head towards the family who are steadfastly ignoring the child. The pain in my head intensifies.

'*Muuuuuuuuum!*'

With my head about to explode I wonder if this is what happens after you've had kids? Do you suddenly become deaf to the noises they make? Does your focus become so sharp that you're able to shut out the whining? What other superpowers are you granted after becoming a parent?

'*Muuuuuuuuuum!*'

The woman *finally* turns around. 'Yes, Lucas.' So, she *can* hear his screaming after all.

'When are we going?' he whines.

'We're going soon,' she tells him.

'But *Muuuuuuuuuum*!'

'Go tell your brothers and bring them back here so you can start packing up your things.'

'But –'

'Now!'

The boy stalks off towards two other boys who are wrestling in the shallows. The woman stands up and takes a phone call, pacing up and down directly in front of me. 'Yes, we're leaving now,' she says, walking left and then right and then left. 'You can put the pasta on and we'll see you soon.' *Can these people even see me?* Apparently not.

Further down the beach three young girls in fluorescent swimsuits are creeping towards a woman lying on a towel. She has a large hat draped over her face and appears to be asleep. The girls stand around the unsuspecting woman, giggling quietly to each other. They silently count to three before launching themselves on top of her, obviously hoping to give her a fright. The woman doesn't flinch. Instead, she slowly pushes her hat to the side, and says something to the girls who race back down the beach. The woman then replaces her hat. I can feel her exhaustion from here.

'Lucas!' The woman who was on the phone is now standing in front of me with her hands on her hips. 'Come here now, otherwise I'm leaving without you.' I realise I never got to find out what happened to the man who was knocked out by the cow.

'But Muuuuuuuuuum!'

'*Lucas!* Now!'

As this conversation continues, I pull out Henri and turn to a blank page. People are obviously not as perfect as I've been making them out to be. In fact, aside from my current state, watching everyone has left me glad and grateful. It's a valuable reminder that nothing is ever the way it appears and we can't possibly know what's going on behind the façades of Saturday morning 'contentment'. Single, married, about to be married, about to be divorced; there are always going to be challenges. No one has a perfect life. Let's face it, at any moment any one of us could be knocked out by a cow.

The words whip across the page as I reflect on the futility of the comparison game. For many years, I didn't think I had it in me to write a book, believing I lacked the discipline and the vocabulary. Stephen King helped me to change this. He said, 'Hedley, you just have to believe in yourself.' Okay, so that's not entirely true. In his book, *On Writing*, he writes, 'One of the really bad things you can do to your writing is to dress up the vocabulary, looking for long words because you're maybe a little bit ashamed of your short ones.' These words were the exact ones I needed to hear.

My art scars had affected my creative confidence. I was self-conscious about the size of my *vocabulary*, believing it to be limited and immature. Or as Mrs Brown might have said, *trite*. I longed to be able to eat from the buffet of big and brilliant words that could light up a page and bring colour and life to a story. Stephen King reminded me that, 'The basic rule of vocabulary is use the first word that comes to your mind if it is appropriate and colourful.'

Letting go of the need for a big vocabulary enabled me to start writing by using the first word that came to mind. My first book had begun. By the time it was finished three years later, I was exhausted, having spent much of that time fighting off the voice in my head that kept telling me I couldn't do it and that I wasn't good enough. I kept writing anyway.

Writing that first book was like climbing a mountain crawling with schoolyard bullies and angry, ex-art teachers whose sole purpose was to destroy my confidence and stop me from reaching the summit. It was one of the hardest things I've ever done. When I finally held a finished copy in my hand, I felt a sense of achievement and an even greater sense of relief. It was an experience I never wanted to go through again. And thankfully I didn't have to. Once your first book is written, it's done. You never have to climb that mountain or believe those voices again.

I look up from Henri and realise I've been lost in my words for over an hour. Interestingly, the scene around me has changed. Hot Furniture Man and his beautiful wife have disappeared along with the other 'happy' twosomes. There's not a couple or family in sight. Instead, they've been replaced by individuals. To my left, a few metres down the beach, a guy wearing a straw hat and sunglasses is leaning against the wall gazing out at the ocean. Further along, a woman lies on her stomach, perched on her elbows, engrossed in a magazine. Directly in front of me a guy is lying on his back holding a book over his face. And to my right, an older man in Speedos is resting on one elbow with a newspaper spread out before him.

One reality has been replaced by an entirely new one. All I did was put my head down for a few minutes and write.

Insight of the Day

Go for a walk. Take off your shoes. Feel the earth. Allow it to touch you, be there for you, heal you, love you. Write with whatever words you have at your disposal. Keep writing until you're done, until you're empty. And remember, no one has a perfect life. We're all just doing our best with what we have.

Day 30

Transformation

I pull up the blanket as tears stream down my cheeks. But these are not the tears of joy and gratitude I'd hoped for at this point. Rather, they're tears of fatigue and illness. When I sat up in bed thirty days ago declaring that I'd write my way back to the person I wanted to be, a burning chest, an ulcerated mouth, cracked lips, raw nostrils, and swollen face were not part of the vision. Nor was feeling sorry for myself.

My thoughts turn to a story in another of Cheryl Strayed's books, *Tiny Beautiful Things*, a collection of letters she wrote to listeners of her radio program, 'Dear Sugar'. In one of the letters, a woman described in horrendous detail the abuse she suffered as a young girl. Now in her thirties, she was struggling to move beyond her grief. Strayed, posing as 'Dear Sugar', didn't censor her response, telling the woman that despite the horrible events that she had endured, no one was coming for her. No one was going to save her, and no one was going to do the work for her. She was going to have to do it herself. Writing the letter was a start but it wasn't enough. This woman was stuck but she was the only one who could get herself unstuck. And the only way to do this was to reach out, ask for help and then grab onto that help for dear life.

I'm stuck and no one is coming for me. I suspect this is what the tears are about. I'm alone, unable to move, and unable to give myself the support I need. And right now I need actual human help. Without it, there's no way I'm going to be able to finish what I've started. And to fail now would represent a new level of heartbreak and disappointment. I grab my phone and text Mum, asking if she can pick me up and take me to the doctor's.

'I don't know how I'm going to get through these last two days,' I tell her an hour or so later as we sit down under a tree on a grassy slope overlooking the beach. It's a clear day with only a few clouds and the mild temperature offers a hint of spring. The antibiotics and painkillers the doctor prescribed have started kicking in.

'You can do it,' says Mum. 'Even if you have to take a break after each sentence.'

'But what am I going to write about? All I can think about is how sick I feel.'

Mum pauses. 'Why not write about mould?'

'Mould?' I laugh and cough at the same time. 'You've got to be kidding.' Mould has been the topic of conversation for much of the morning. I found quite a lot of it in my bedroom cupboard and started wondering if it might have contributed to my illness. 'Mould isn't exactly an enticing topic. What's there to write about?'

'Mould ruled my life when I was living in Italy,' Mum says.

A few years after my parents divorced, my mother moved to Italy for five months to study Italian.

'In what way?' I ask.

'The apartment I was living in had a lot of moisture on the walls.

The owner had asked if I could keep the windows open even though it was the middle of winter and snowing. He would come by the apartment to check and when he saw signs of mould, he started yelling at me. He told me it was my fault and said I had to leave. It was horrible.'

'That's awful. What did you do?'

'Well, I learnt how to argue in Italian! But then I had to start looking around for somewhere else to live, which wasn't easy. I was on my own in a foreign country. I didn't know anyone and I was still a novice with the language. Looking back, I wonder why I didn't just pack it in and come home.'

'Why didn't you?'

'One afternoon, I was walking through town when I bumped into the man's wife. She asked how I was going and I told her what had happened. She said, "Leave it with me. I'll fix it." I didn't think she'd do anything. She must have noticed the disbelief on my face because she looked me in the eyes and said, "*Fidati di me*", trust me. When I got home that night there was a letter of apology from the owner and a bottle of wine.'

'Wow. That's amazing. I wonder what she said to him.'

'I'm not sure. But there were rumours flying around that he was having an affair and the wife knew. I suspect she laid down the law and he didn't have much choice other than to go along with it. That's my guess, anyway. I could be wrong.'

'So what happened after that?'

'I stayed in the apartment. The mould problem continued but it didn't bother me as much as it did the owner.'

'Did you ever see him again?'

Mum nods. 'I saw him walking through town one day but he pretended not to see me. He looked very sheepish.'

I laugh. 'I didn't expect that story to come from mould.'

'You can find a story in anything if you want to.'

I wonder whether mould could be yet another metaphor. I type the word into my dream dictionary.

Mould: *To see mould in your dream indicates that something in your life has been ignored or is no longer of any use. It may also refer to the negative emotions that are expanding and growing in your subconscious. You need to find a productive way to express them before it gets out of control. Alternatively, the mould may also represent transformation.*

The last sentence captures my attention. *The mould may also represent transformation.* An insight begins slowly unwrapping itself. I've been treating this illness like it's a burden, a misfortune. But what if it isn't? What if it's a manifestation of something else, such as a letting go of something that's no longer of use? What if it's just my body's way of ridding itself of whatever it no longer requires? What if this illness is a good thing, as in the final stages of a transformation which I've been undertaking throughout this last month?

I feel a sudden surge of energy. It's the confirmation I needed. Mum was right.

—

Back home I curl up on the couch in front of the TV having decided this would be the perfect time to watch *Wild*, the movie based on Cheryl Strayed's book. Towards the end of the film, an image flashes up on the screen. I lurch forward on the couch. The image appears for less than a split second but I know I've seen it before. And yet I can't have seen it before as this is the first time I've seen the movie. Confused, I grab the remote and press rewind. The shot is of Reese Witherspoon as Cheryl covered in tiny, jumping frogs. Without thinking, I grab my computer and flick back to Day 7.

I dreamt of frogs last night. Lots of them. Tiny, slimy, bouncing frogs.

The image on the screen in front of me is the same picture I saw in my dream. Yet instead of the frogs jumping over Cheryl they were jumping over me. I continue reading what I wrote.

To see leaping frogs in your dream indicates your lack of commitment.

This doesn't make sense. If the frogs symbolise commitment, why would they be showing up now? Sure, I can understand why they might have shown up during that first week but I've since proven my capacity for commitment. I've been more committed to this project than I have to anything in a long time. There has to be some mistake. I must have misunderstood or missed something. I return to the dream dictionary. Sure enough, there's more to the definition.

Frogs (cont.): *Frogs also represent a potential for change or the unexpected. The frog may be a prince in disguise and thus signify transformation, renewal or rebirth.*

Somehow I missed this extra bit of the definition. And perhaps for good reason. At the time, I was lacking commitment. Yet a change *has* occurred. Lots of changes have occurred, yet these changes would not have been possible without overcoming the obstacles (frogs?) along the way, including this illness. What if each of these obstacles were actually a prince in disguise, thus signifying the transformation, renewal and rebirth?

Insight of the Day

Obstacles are just a prince charming in disguise.

Day 31

A new beginning

Searching through the chest of drawers in my bedroom, my fingers land on a white plastic object. My heart quickens as I'm transported back to that night in February more than five months ago. The object – a plastic disposable mouthpiece about the size of the palm of your hand – was left behind by the ambulance officers who found me unconscious on my bedroom floor. I keep it as a reminder not only of what happened that night but of the choice I made: to live.

When I first discovered the mouthpiece a few days after coming home from hospital, it prompted a series of questions. What happened after I called the ambulance? How long did it take for it to arrive? Who found me? Where did they find me? What position was I in? What did they do to me? Why did they need the mouthpiece? What did they do with it? Why was it in my bedroom? Why didn't they take it with them? From the moment I passed out to the moment I woke up in intensive care, I had nothing but questions.

A few days after returning home, while sitting at the kitchen table with Anna, there was a knock on the door. It was after eight on a Thursday night. I looked over at Anna, wondering who it could be since I wasn't expecting any other visitors. When I opened the door, I didn't recognise the man standing there. He was well built and ruggedly handsome, dressed in white T-shirt, jeans and thongs. He was holding some folded pieces of paper. While I didn't recognise him, he seemed to know me and introduced himself as 'Dave'. All of a sudden something clicked. This was the ambulance officer who'd found me.

After he confirmed my assumption, I eagerly invited him inside, insisting he join us for some tea. 'You saved my life,' I told him. He shrugged it off as if it were no big deal. I continued to thank him profusely before remembering my many unanswered questions.

Dave was shy and spoke softly. 'When we arrived the place was locked up. We knocked, but obviously you couldn't hear us. I came around the side and looked through your bedroom window. You were lying face down on the floor. We couldn't tell if you were alive at this point but, we knew if you were, the position you were lying in was dangerous because your airwaves would be blocked. You were at risk of suffocating.'

I swallowed hard and signalled for him to keep going.

'We were about to call the police and get them to come and break one of the windows. We're not allowed to do it ourselves because we'd be putting our lives at risk so, by law, if we can't get into a property we have to call the police. Then I saw one of your bedroom windows was open, so we climbed in. You were still breathing.'

Tears welled in my eyes.

'We tried to get a trachea into your airwaves but you pushed back, you wouldn't let us put it in.'

'I wouldn't?' I said, half-laughing, half on the verge of crying. 'Not the best time to be difficult.'

'Actually, it was a good sign. You didn't want our help. You wanted to breathe on your own. We got you in the ambulance and then got you to hospital as quickly as possible. You were very lucky. I checked your bathroom and found the empty bottle of Valium. I figured you must have swallowed the lot.'

I nodded, looking down at the table. I didn't know what to say. Words felt inadequate, and my brain still wasn't working properly.

'We see this all the time and more often than not the outcome isn't good,' Dave went on. 'Often these people are pretty messed up, they have drug and alcohol addictions or they're just down and out, but with you ... Well, I just couldn't work it out.'

I shook my head. There was so much I wanted to say but simply couldn't. I didn't have the words or the energy. Instead, I looked at the pile of papers Dave had brought with him.

'Oh,' he said, sliding them across the table. 'I wanted to give this back.'

'What is it?' I asked, confused.

Dave shifted in his chair. 'When we come across situations like yours, we always look for any clues or hints that might help piece together what happened –'

'You mean like a suicide note?' I asked. Dave nodded. 'But I didn't write a suicide note.'

'I know. Although I didn't at the time. When I was looking around your room, I found these papers lying on top of your dresser. I took them thinking they might explain what you'd done but when I took a look I realised ... anyway, I thought I should bring them back.'

I had no idea what he was talking about. I took a look and suddenly remembered. 'Oh my God!' I said, covering my mouth. I could feel my face turning beetroot. 'Did you read this?'

Dave nodded. 'Sorry. I didn't mean to but once I got started, I couldn't stop. It's ... good.'

'What is it?' asked Anna.

'It's the outline for an erotic novel,' I said. 'A very *graphic* erotic novel.' I'd started it six months earlier only to stop when the story became challenging. I walked away from it, just as I had done so many times before, at the point it became hard. Of course, I didn't know then what I know now.

Anna laughed, grabbing the papers from me. I watched as her eyes raced across the pages, her expression suggesting she understood what I meant. 'Whoa.'

I turned to Dave, my face still crimson. 'I can't believe you read the outline for my erotic novel thinking it was a *suicide note*. You must have been surprised.'

Dave laughed. 'I always prepare myself to expect the unexpected but I have to say I wasn't expecting *that*. Anyway, I wanted to return it and to let you know I think you're a good writer. You should keep going.'

—

I smile now, remembering Dave's words. The Universe certainly does have a sense of humour, even in the darkest of moments. Back then I hadn't registered I wasn't writing on a regular basis. I didn't realise how that affected my mental and emotional state. It's only now, having finished this creative pilgrimage, that I am able to recognise just how important writing is. Every word I've written has been like a drop of medicine, healing my heart and mind by reconnecting them with my soul.

This pilgrimage wasn't just about writing two thousand words a day. It was about reminding myself of who I am and what I'm capable of. Writing is what I love. It's what my soul longs for. Somewhere along the way I forgot this. I got distracted, seeking other people's approval and validation. I forgot how much pleasure writing gives me. I forgot the sense of peace that arises and how my heart purrs and my soul smiles. I forgot how writing helps me to make sense of the world and my place in it. I forgot that if I stop writing, life stops making sense. That's when I start asking dangerous questions like, 'What's the point?' That's when I stop thinking and instead swallow enough pills to snuff out my light for good.

I knew something had to change and that something had to be me. No one was coming for me and no one was going to do it for me. Nor was it anyone's job. It was up to me to turn my life around even if it meant bush-bashing my way back to whatever was my truth. To do that, I needed a challenge. And writing two thousand words a day for a month was it. Having never done it before, I didn't know if I *could* do it. I just knew I needed to.

I remember the fear that first morning after making the commitment. *Have I just set myself up to fail again? What will happen if I do? What if I give up halfway through? What if I can't even manage a month of writing every day? Then who am I?*

Not a single day has gone by when I thought, *I've got this in the bag.* Fear remained my constant companion, especially during those first two weeks. I had to take it one day at a time and greet each morning as separate from the last. I knew if I fell too far forward into the future or too far back into the past, I'd risk losing the state of presence necessary to finish. Complacency could be fatal. It had almost been once before. I didn't want to take that risk again. I needed to stay alert, present and focused.

Thankfully I did. The shambolic state of my apartment is proof! Jumbled pairs of shoes line the hallway, crumpled towels cover the bathroom floor, unpaid bills litter the kitchen table and dishes are stacked high in the sink. I haven't quite found the balance yet. It's no big deal. These things can be cleaned and fixed and dealt with. Sometimes life needs to get messy to create order and structure. It's a work in progress, after all.

I always thought to be creative you had to be a free-flowing and whimsical artist, floating from one idea or experiment to the next. But that's only part of it. A creative is all of these things, but she's also an arse-kicking warrior who shows up no matter what because that's what free-loving, arse-kicking warrior artists do. Creativity is faith *as well as* follow-through. It's both whimsical *and* disciplined; carefree *and* courageous; flexible *and* fierce. It's an expression of both sides of the same coin; that coin being *life*.

Before this adventure began, there were certain words I would never have associated with the creative path. Words like commitment, ambition, determination, sacrifice, courage, persistence, structure, focus, consistency, integrity, mental toughness, emotional awareness, compassion and forgiveness. Creativity is a playground but, like all playgrounds, it needs structure and boundaries. This was surprising and unexpected. We need to have space to play and explore and create, but too much space can leave us paralysed.

The urge to create is a natural one. We are products of creation. It's who we are at the core of our being. How our souls want to express this true nature becomes a process of self (or soul?) discovery. And sometimes the proverbial shit has to hit the fan before we finally give ourselves the time and space, along with the permission, to create. Ideally, not so much shit that we end up in hospital.

We are all artists, even those of us who say 'I don't have a creative bone in my body'. Whether it's writing a screenplay, designing a house, making it beautiful, acting out a scene, making a coffee, building a café, playing the guitar, or colouring in with an orange pencil, we are all in the process of making something that wasn't there before. We don't need a reason to do this. Just the act of being creative is reason enough. Being creative is a reminder of who we are beyond our human form.

Creativity reminded me that no one cares whether I write or not.

This is not a personal put-down. It's a fact. The world won't stop turning if I don't write. But for *my* world to keep turning I *have* to write. I have to keep picking up my notebook and pen. It keeps me grounded and connected. It gives me meaning and purpose. If I can turn what I write into something others enjoy, that's a bonus. But it's not the reason I write. It can't be.

With these insights tucked into my heart's pocket, I move through Day 31 with gratitude. Not just for having made it to the end, but also for the many and varied 'messengers' – both two-legged and four-legged – who showed up along the way. Each one played an important role in getting me to this point. There was Christian, the screenwriter from the first day, who reminded me that success doesn't have to be complicated and to believe in my own potential as a writer. Emma and Brett took the idea for a creative pilgrimage and made it their own with 'Sexy September'. Unfortunately, they collapsed from utter exhaustion in the first week, but at least they gave it a go. My friend Grace invited me to the theatre on several occasions where I learnt to make up my mind and stick to it. Cleo made me laugh with her story about turning up to a black-tie event dressed as a martini glass, reminding me of the importance of taking creative risks and standing by them. There was Boris, the Russian chiropractor, who connected pictures of a bear and her cub with the message that life is a teacher and it will always provide us with the teaching we require. Even though that might be uncomfortable and inconvenient, it's necessary.

My dear friend Anna, talented interior designer, offered the support and encouragement when I needed it most. She introduced me to Fine & Sonny where I met the shop assistant who inspired me to get up earlier. Her colleagues reminded me of the importance of always telling a story with the audience in mind. Rhett, my actor and writer friend, decided to finish writing his play regardless of his fear of failure. He helped me recognise my own fear of endings and the importance of having another project to look forward to, so as not to lose the creative momentum. Mr World War II reminded me to smile and to not take this whole writing thing too seriously; to have fun with it; and to remember how lucky I am to be able to call myself a writer. Graeme Simsion taught me to write the best book I can possibly write and not let anything get in the way of that. Fiona McIntosh pointed out there are no excuses for not writing. And even though there are, in fact, many excuses to not write, she reminded me not to listen to any of those excuses and to keep writing regardless.

Matt, the owner of Smith's, told me that 'nothing good comes without a little sacrifice' and propelled me towards a new understanding and relationship with the word and concept. I discovered that sacrifice wasn't about giving something up, but making it holy. I realised I could sacrifice guilt and procrastination, which is preferable to sacrificing coffee or chocolate. When I was struck down by an infection, Mum gave me the support and help I needed that enabled me to finish this thing. And there was Cheryl Strayed, who by writing and sharing her story, inspired me to write and share mine.

But it wasn't just the people; there were the dolphins and whales, kookaburras and frogs, who showed up at the perfect time with their silent, and sometimes not so silent, messages and insights.

I'm grateful to everyone and everything who played a part. Without them I wouldn't have the insights and the understandings I now have, I wouldn't be the writer I've now become. This pilgrimage has enabled me to wander down paths, share experiences, and connect with countless different people. But ultimately this pilgrimage has brought me home. That is, back to myself. When I began, I thought 'home' was on the 'other side', in another realm. It was the 'place' from where I came and to which I was returning once my life was over. I didn't swallow those pills because I wanted to die. I wanted to go 'home'. This yearning was palpable, but it was also misguided. Home is not on the 'other' side. Home isn't my apartment, or the house I grew up in, or the city where I was born or the country in which I live. Home is where I am, right now, in this moment. I am home because I *am* my home.

While this might be the end of this particular story, this is not the end. Thankfully. Tomorrow I have the privilege of rising, early of course, and starting a new day. And a new story. For now, I'm just happy to be home.

Insight of the Day

Being creative is a reminder of who we are. A daily creative practice is a daily reminder. May we always remember the truth of our being and listen to the callings of our soul. May we always be grateful for the opportunity to live on this earth, in this body, and make the most of the glorious luxury to live as a creative being.

Epilogue

The day after I finished this creative pilgrimage, I learnt that one of my favourite authors, Dr Wayne Dyer, had died. The news shocked me. Dr Dyer had been in Australia only the week before speaking at an event in Melbourne. He'd been diagnosed with leukaemia in 2009 but tragically died of a heart attack. When I found out, I went looking for more information and came across a blog post titled *A Gift in the Storm* (also an excerpt from his book, *I Can See Clearly Now*). In the excerpt he writes of his separation from his wife in 2001 and how it left him profoundly depressed and unable to write. He would sleep for long stretches, lacking the motivation to do much else. Not interested in eating, he lost weight and had to force himself to go outside for his daily run. His children (he had eight!) were understandably worried and suggested he start writing again.

Inspired by both his children and a quote from Carlos Castaneda's book *The Power of Silence*, Dr Dyer had an epiphany and dedicated the next year to writing every single day. Through this experience, he describes coming out of the sadness that had enveloped him, feeling more compassion for himself, and rediscovering his purpose. He sensed the 'presence of God' as 'the field of intent' and that it was this 'presence' doing the writing that got him through. He acknowledges how the pain and heartbreak following the separation made him a 'more tender and empathetic writer'.

All this was news to me. I didn't know his greatest love was writing even though he wrote over thirty books, many of them international bestsellers. I thought his books were simply vehicles for him to convey his spiritual messages. Writing had brought me back from the brink yet I was surprised to learn it also had done the same for Dr Dyer. But then this is the power of creativity.

—

It's now over a year since I finished the creative pilgrimage and the 'first words' of this manuscript. The benefits continue to reveal themselves in varying and mysterious ways. As I write this epilogue, I'm sitting in a bustling café in Crouch End, a quaint suburb in North London where I'm visiting a friend for her fortieth birthday. Naturally, my table is against a brick wall at the rear of the café from where I'm able to observe the morning's action. Two women wrapped in their winter jackets stand at the door as waiters and conversations swirl around them. Outside, the day is cloaked in the drab greyness of an English winter.

My creative pilgrimage changed my life. My relationship with creativity is stronger than ever and, as a result, so am I. While I'm not writing two thousand words a day anymore, I'm putting pen to page almost every day and I'm all the better for it. Usually I come down with a cold at least once a year, sometimes more than once. Since finishing the pilgrimage, I've been healthy. I'm convinced this is due to the transformation that occurred during those thirty-one days.

Emotionally, I'm also stronger. Of course, life still throws up challenges, but I no longer feel like I can't meet them. I no longer want 'out'. In those moments when everything seems 'too hard', I remind myself to 'write my way home'. This has become a mantra. Whatever the struggle, writing draws me out of it and brings me back to myself. I always feel better after putting pen to paper. This is where I'm able to make sense of the non-sense. Writing is how I find my way home when I get lost.

As for my relationship with that erotic novel I started, things didn't quite work out. It was going well until I hit the forty-thousand-word mark. I decided it wasn't going anywhere and it was time to break up. This was nothing to despair about. I simply moved on to the next story and kept writing. I'm currently halfway through a new book and I'm in the planning stages for the one after that. The process may not have cured me of the urge to fling myself at the next shiny new idea, but it's pulled the urge back into line.

I've given up trying to write the 'perfect' book. There's no such thing, so it's pointless to even try. As Graeme Simsion said, 'Write the best book you can write.' For me, the best book is not a perfect one. I could spend my life working on this manuscript, tightening it and making it better, but that would take a lifetime and there are too many other ideas and stories I want to tell. I can, however, write the best book I can possibly write.

I wholeheartedly recommend a creative pilgrimage, especially if you're feeling lost or stuck and wondering if there's more. There is. It can be found through a regular creative practice. It doesn't have to be writing. It can be anything at all; as long as it's something that excites you. If you're not sure what this is, ask yourself, what did I love doing as a child? What were my favourite subjects at school? What did I wish I could do more of if I had the time? Whatever it is, do it every day for thirty-one days and see what happens. I can guarantee something *will* happen and chances are it'll be wonderful – and what you least expect.

The Prayer of Saint Francis

Lord, make me an instrument of your peace.
Where there is hatred, let me sow love;
Where there is injury, pardon;
Where there is doubt, faith;
Where there is despair, hope;
Where there is darkness, light;
Where there is sadness, joy.

O Divine Master, grant that I may not so much seek
To be consoled as to console;
To be understood as to understand;
To be loved as to love.
For it is in giving that we receive;
It is in pardoning that we are pardoned;
And it is in dying to self that we are born to eternal life.

Ithaka

Constantine P. Cavafy

As you set out for Ithaka
hope the voyage is a long one,
full of adventure, full of discovery.
Laistrygonians and Cyclops,
angry Poseidon—don't be afraid of them:
you'll never find things like that on your way
as long as you keep your thoughts raised high,
as long as a rare excitement
stirs your spirit and your body.
Laistrygonians and Cyclops,
wild Poseidon—you won't encounter them
unless you bring them along inside your soul,
unless your soul sets them up in front of you.

Hope the voyage is a long one.
May there be many a summer morning when,
with what pleasure, what joy,
you come into harbors seen for the first time;
may you stop at Phoenician trading stations
to buy fine things,
mother of pearl and coral, amber and ebony,
sensual perfume of every kind—
as many sensual perfumes as you can;
and may you visit many Egyptian cities
to gather stores of knowledge from their scholars.

Keep Ithaka always in your mind.
Arriving there is what you are destined for.
But do not hurry the journey at all.
Better if it lasts for years,
so you are old by the time you reach the island,
wealthy with all you have gained on the way,
not expecting Ithaka to make you rich.

Ithaka gave you the marvellous journey.
Without her you would not have set out.
She has nothing left to give you now.

And if you find her poor, Ithaka won't have fooled you.
Wise as you will have become, so full of experience,
you will have understood by then what these Ithakas mean.

Select Bibliography

Currey, M. *Daily Rituals: How Great Minds Make Time, Find Inspiration, and Get to Work*. New York: Knopf, 2013

Derenzie, H. *Creative Keynote: 7 Keys to Public Speaking Artistry for Creative Professionals*. Sydney: Pinecone Publishing, 2014

Derenzie, H. *Finding Paris: An Unusual Love Story*. Sydney: Pinecone Publishing, 2013

Dyer, W. *I Can See Clearly Now.* California: Hay House, 2014

Dyer, W. *Inspiration: Your Ultimate Calling*. California: Hay House, 2006

King, S. *On Writing: A Memoir of the Craft.* New York: Scribner, 2000

Pressfield, S. *The War of Art: Break Through the Blocks & Win Your Inner Creative Battles.* New York: Warner Books, 2002

Strayed, C. *Wild: From Lost to Found on the Pacific Crest Trail.* New York: Knopf, 2012

Acknowledgments

My heartfelt thanks to everyone who helped to make this book possible including, but not limited to Anne Looby, Anna-Carin McNamara, Julie Wood, Danita Serina, Malcolm Beville, Marcel, Bob Selden, Michael Ferrara, Vicki Tennant, Jackie Evans, Bryony Sutherland, and my mother, Di Derenzie. A very special thank you to Rod and Tegan Morrison from Brio Books who brought my book to life.